Budgeting for Disarmament: The Costs of War and Peace

MICHAEL RENNER

WORLDWATCH PAPER 122
November 1994

FINANCIAL SUPPORT is provided by the Geraldine R. Dodge Foundation, W. Alton Jones Foundation, John D. and Catherine T. MacArthur Foundation, Andrew W. Mellon Foundation, Curtis and Edith Munson Foundation, Edward John Noble Foundation, Pew Charitable Trusts, Lynn R. and Karl E. Prickett Fund, Rockefeller Brothers Fund, Surdna Foundation, Turner Foundation, Frank Weeden Foundation, Wallace Genetic Foundation, and Peter Buckley.

PUBLICATIONS of the Institute include the annual *State of the World*, which is now published in 27 languages; *Vital Signs*, an annual compendium of the global trends—environmental, economic, and social—that are shaping our future; the *Environmental Alert* book series; and *World Watch* magazine, as well as the *Worldwatch Papers*. For more information on Worldwatch publications, write: Worldwatch Institute, 1776 Massachusetts Ave., N.W., Washington, DC 20036; or FAX (202) 296-7365.

THE WORLDWATCH PAPERS provide in-depth, quantitative and qualitative analysis of the major issues affecting prospects for a sustainable society. The Papers are authored by members of the Worldwatch Institute research staff and reviewed by experts in the field. Published in five languages, they have been used as a concise and authoritative reference by governments, nongovernmental organizations and educational institutions worldwide. For a partial list of available Papers, see page 71.

DATA from all graphs and tables contained in this book, as well as from those in all other Worldwatch publications of the past year, are available on diskette for use with Macintosh or IBM-compatible computers. This includes data from the *State of the World* series, *Vital Signs* series, Worldwatch Papers, *World Watch* magazine, and the *Environmental Alert* series. The data are formatted for use with spreadsheet software compatible with Lotus 1-2-3, including Quattro Pro, Excel, SuperCalc, and many others. Both 3 1/2" and 5 1/4" diskettes are supplied. To order, send check or money order for $89, or credit card number and expiration date (Visa and MasterCard only), to Worldwatch Institute, 1776 Massachusetts Ave., NW, Washington, DC 20036. Tel: 202-452-1999; Fax: 202-296-7365; Internet: wwpub@igc.apc.org.

Table of Contents

Tables and Figures

ACKNOWLEDGMENTS: I would like to thank Nicole Ball, Ken Epps, Herbert Wulf, and my colleagues at the Worldwatch Institute for their comments on earlier drafts of this document, and Lori Baldwin for providing research assistance. I would also like to thank my wife and children for the inspiration that made long hours of research and writing seem worthwhile.

MICHAEL RENNER is a Senior Researcher at the Worldwatch Institute. He is the author of *Economic Adjustments After the Cold War: Strategies for Conversion* (1992), a book commissioned by the United Nations Institute for Disarmament Research, and a co-author of the Institute's annual *State of the World* reports. His most recent previous Worldwatch Paper, *Critical Juncture: The Future of Peacekeeping*, was published in May 1993. He holds degrees in international relations and political science from the Universities of Amsterdam, Netherlands, and Konstanz, Germany.

Introduction: A New Indicator

When the Soviet Union and United States halted their half-century-long Cold War at the end of the 1980s, the global news media were suddenly filled with talk of an anticipated "peace dividend"—an historic opportunity for governments all over the world to recast their priorities from war and war preparation toward disarmament and neglected civilian needs and endeavors. With this reorientation, substantial savings would occur from *not* spending as much money on the military as in previous decades.[1]

The cover of the *Human Development Report 1994*, published by the United Nations Development Programme (UNDP), illustrates this expectation: depicting what looks like a stylized staircase, it shows the evolution of global military expenditures in past years and projections for future years, with a steady and ultimately significant decline.[2]

The world's total military spending has indeed declined—from $995 billion to an estimated $767 billion between 1987 and 1994. The cumulative reduction, arrived at by adding the annual savings compared to the 1987 spending figure, has amounted to some $935 billion—roughly equivalent to a year's worth of expenditures. Still, reality has not quite matched the optimistic expectations. The cutbacks have been relatively small compared to the epochal political transformations the world witnessed in the late 1980s. Today, military budgets are still as high as they were in the late 1970s, when U.S.-Soviet détente came to an end. Military spending is "stuck" at a fairly high level, and may not decline substantially more. Herbert Wulf, director of the Bonn International Center for Conversion, has pointedly remarked that "to do a little less of the same is the overriding principle of governments' policy."[3]

Western governments, instead of deliberately reallocating freed-up budgetary resources from the military to the civilian realm, have largely preferred to reduce deficits or offer tax cuts. Meanwhile, although the former Warsaw Pact states have slashed their military budgets, the profound and crisis-laden transformations of their economies have yielded investment deficits rather than surpluses. Several developing countries have curtailed their military spending, but in large parts of the Third World peace remains elusive. In East Asia, governments are taking advantage of booming economies to build their military muscle. In the Middle East, even the unfolding Arab-Israeli peace is not expected to lower arms spending. It is true that deficit reductions and tax cuts occasioned by military cuts provide some economic benefits. But the peace dividend as originally envisioned has largely failed to materialize, disappearing instead into a gigantic fiscal Bermuda Triangle.[4]

The initial post-Cold War euphoria and the hope for peace around the globe quickly evaporated in the face of large-scale conflict in the Persian Gulf. Although a number of protracted conflicts have come to an end, they have been quickly replaced by a seemingly endless stream of new battles—some of them long-standing conflicts erupting again after a hiatus. According to the Stockholm International Peace Research Institute, the number of major wars—those that kill at least 1,000 persons—rose to 34 in 1993, after having dropped from 36 in 1987 to 30 in 1991. And an analysis including "lesser" wars shows a steady upward trend throughout the period since the end of World War II.[5]

The post-Cold War era presents a mix of peril and promise—and hence both a need and an opportunity for a new peace policy. But in the face of this challenge, there is a palpable lack of strategic vision or leadership toward a truly new world order, an inertia that leaves policymakers stuck in traditional modes of thinking and relying on outdated policy tools.

The demilitarization imperative is three-fold. The first challenge is to assist countries emerging from the devastation of warfare in their efforts to rebuild and fashion viable civil societies and economies less susceptible to breakdown and strife. The second is to slash the enormous arsenals of destruction accumulated over decades; to adopt meaningful restrictions on arms production, possession, and trade; and to convert war-making capacities to civilian use. Finally—and this is likely to be the greatest challenge—there is a need to create institutions that are capable of robust peacekeeping, nonviolent dispute resolution, and war prevention. (See Table 1.)

How much progress is the world making toward building the foundations of peace? A crucial indicator is found in the resources that governments and international organizations are making available to accomplish those tasks. Throughout the Cold War, when a nation's or an alliance's coercive and deterrent power was considered central to maintaining its security, military spending was a key indicator. But there is growing recognition that security in an interdependent world requires cooperation, not confrontation, and that social equality, economic vitality, and environmental stability are more important to a country's fortunes than martial qualities.

Arms control and disarmament, demobilization of armed forces, and peacekeeping have indeed become far more important than they were at any time during the past half-century; they have moved from rhetoric to reality. But if these endeavors and the resources devoted to them are to be more than palliatives, peace-making institutions will need to replace war-making institutions, and peace and disarmament spending will replace military spending as a key indicator.

To be ultimately successful, a comprehensive peace policy needs to combine measures that address the symptoms of conflict—the institutions and arsenals of the war system—with those that address the roots of conflict—the accelerating social, economic, and environmental pressures that cause unemployment, poverty, and dislocation and that set different communities, classes, and countries on a collision course with each other in a struggle for resources and survival. Working to reduce these pressures and to overcome the inequities and divisions that are likely triggers of conflict will be a continual challenge for local, national, and international policymakers.

TABLE 1

The Scope of the Demilitarization and Peacebuilding Challenge

RESTITUTION
(Coping with the Legacy of War)
  Reconstruction
  Land mine clearance
  Environmental cleanup
  Refugee repatriation
  Demobilization and reintegration of ex-combatants

TRANSFORMATION
(Moving from War to Peace)
  Decommissioning and dismantling of arms
  Bans or restrictions on arms production and trade
  Treaty verification (monitoring/inspections)
  Base closures
  Conversion of military production facilities, bases, and land

PEACEBUILDING
(Building Peacekeeping and Peacemaking Institutions)
  Peacekeeping
  Conflict early-warning system
  Conflict resolution/mediation
  Strengthened international legal system (World Court, International
    Criminal Court, War Tribunals)
  Sanctions support fund
  Peace research and education

Costs of War, Costs of Peace

In this era of cost-cutting and belt-tightening, the focus seems to have shifted from the peace dividend to concern about the "costs of peace"—as if peace were perhaps unaffordable. At the same time that a considerable number of expensive military programs continue to be pursued or are newly initiated, peace and disarmament-related expenditures are subjected to a nickle-and-dime scrutiny.[6]

For example, expenditures for United Nations peacekeeping operations are often portrayed as "exorbitant" in Western countries, even though the world's governments still spend some $250 on their militaries for each $1 invested in peacekeeping. Senator John McCain, opposing the Clinton administration's proposal to fund a portion of U.S. peacekeeping dues from the Pentagon budget, declared in June 1994 that "if we choose now to identify the defense budget as the cash cow" for U.N. peacekeeping operations, "we are setting the stage for the demise of [military] readiness and dooming our [armed] services to operate with even more austere resources than are offered under the current gutted defense budget." The proposed funding, some $300 million, was defeated in Congress; it would have been equivalent to about 0.1 percent of the U.S. military budget for 1995.[7]

There are numerous examples of governments keeping not only peacekeeping but also disarmament and post-conflict reconstruction on a short financial leash. Governments agreed on a convention outlawing chemical weapons, but decided to cut to the bone the budget for establishing the organization that is supposed to verify worldwide compliance with the treaty. And donors' grand pledges to aid Cambodia, El Salvador, Mozambique, and other war-ravaged countries in their efforts to reconstruct, clear landmines, and demobilize combatants are rarely matched by their actual assistance.

Full-cost accounting would make it abundantly clear that "national security" through ever increasing military prowess carries a prohibitive pricetag.

Peace obviously has its costs. But in judging the expenditures associated with demilitarization and peacebuilding efforts, the distinction between costs of war and those of peace is crucial. Many of the bills now coming due—such as those to decontaminate military bases—are in effect the financial after-shocks of decades of war and war preparation. They will be incurred regardless of whether humanity succeeds in fashioning an alternative system to handle conflicts within and among countries. But if an alternative does not materialize, these aftershocks will keep recurring.

In environmental affairs, health care, and other issues, there is growing recognition that an ounce of prevention is worth a pound of cure. The same generally holds true for war and peace. Full-cost accounting, long overdue, would make it abundantly clear that "national security" through ever increasing military prowess carries a prohibitive pricetag.

The costs imposed by the war system are manifold. They begin with the resources needed just to maintain it. Global military spending since World War II has added up to a cumulative $30-35 trillion. The military sector absorbs substantial resources that could help reduce the potential for violent conflict if they were invested instead in human security—health, housing, education, poverty eradication, and environmental sustainability. For example, the price paid for two warships ordered by Malaysia from a British company in 1992 would have provided safe drinking water for the next quarter century to the 5 million Malaysians now lacking it.[8]

The costs of war also entail the expense of getting rid of accumulated arsenals, either by the routine scrapping of obsolete stocks or via measures to comply with international arms treaties. Those costs encompass the outlays required to decontaminate and rehabilitate land and facilities used to produce, test, and maintain weapons and to preserve combat readiness. And they obviously include costs that arise from warfare's destruction and dislocation—the physical and ecological damage, the loss of harvests and industrial production, the uprooting of populations and the resulting need for humanitarian assistance and refugee resettlement, and, eventually, the reconstruction efforts. (See Table 2.) Indications are that in each of these categories, the costs run at least in the tens and possibly the hundreds of billions of dollars globally.[9]

In contrast, the costs of building a robust peace system are likely to be much more modest. Creating an effective multilateral peacekeeping system, curbing or banning much of the production and trade of armaments (and coming up with effective means to verify compliance), developing mechanisms to recognize conflicts before they erupt into violence, providing means for peaceful settlements, strengthening the rule of international law—these are endeavors that can legitimately be

TABLE 2
Economic Costs of War, Selected Examples

Region/Years	Observation
Iran-Iraq 1980-88	The war cost an estimated $416 billion just up to 1985—including money to conduct the war, the damage sustained, the oil revenues forgone, and the GNP lost. This figure surpasses the two countries' combined earnings of $364 billion from oil sales since they first started exporting petroleum.
Persian Gulf 1990-91	According to the Arab Monetary Fund, the Iraqi occupation of Kuwait and the war to reverse it cost the region some $676 billion. This includes the direct costs of the war and the damage it inflicted, and economic impacts such as the loss of earnings, but not the vast environmental damage.
Central America 1980-89	Estimates of direct and indirect war losses total $1.1 billion in El Salvador and $2.5 billion in Nicaragua (including the cost of the U.S. embargo). The costs for rehabilitation of land and equipment are not included.
Southern Africa 1980-88	Economic costs of South African acts of destabilization and aggression are estimated at $27-30 billion for Angola and about $15 billion for Mozambique.

Sources: Michael Renner, "Iran-Iraq War Produces Only Losers," *World Watch*, November/December 1988; Youssef M. Ibrahim, "War Is Said to Cost the Persian Gulf $676 Billion in 1990 and '91," *New York Times*, April 25, 1993; Benjamin L. Crosby, "Central America," and Mark C. Chona and Jeffrey I. Herbst, "Southern Africa," both in Anthony Lake et al., *After the Wars: Reconstruction in Afghanistan, Indochina, Central America, Southern Africa, and the Horn of Africa* (New Brunswick, N.J.: Transaction Publishers for Overseas Development Council, 1990).

regarded as costs of peace. If governments were to pursue the building of a peace system with the same seriousness as they built military muscle, in all likelihood many violent conflicts could be avoided.

A comparatively small investment—perhaps $20-30 billion per year—could make a tremendous difference in the global war and peace balance. The upfront costs of building and making the transition to a peace system ought to be regarded not as an unwelcome expense but as an overdue investment. In the long run, the benefits—in financial savings and in human lives—would clearly be dominant. Not making these investments will condemn humanity to bear the costs of the war system *ad infinitum.*

Distinguishing between war and peace costs does not imply a choice between pursuing one or the other. A lasting peace cannot be built without dealing with the remnants of the war system. Given the huge stocks of military equipment around the globe, it is difficult to imagine that antagonists will rely on non-violent means of settling disputes. Hence, far-reaching disarmament is a prerequisite for peacebuilding. And converting military facilities to civilian use and developing viable civilian employment alternatives are essential to diminishing the economic imperative for the continued large-scale production and export of military equipment.

Conversely, addressing only the immediate symptoms of the war system without tackling its roots will likely condemn humanity to repeat its past experience. Governments may now balk at the costs of conflict prevention and peacebuilding, but failure to set in motion the transition from a war system to a peace system will impose far greater costs. It is far cheaper, and far more preferable, to try to avoid violent conflict than to cope with its repercussions—massive outpourings of refugees and humanitarian emergencies.

The annual expenditures of the United Nations High Commissioner for Refugees (UNHCR), for example, have soared almost 100-fold—from $12 million in the early 1970s to almost $1.1 billion in 1993. In just the first nine months of 1993, the U.N. Department of Humanitarian Affairs, responsible for coordinating humanitarian programs of different U.N. agencies, launched 17 "consolidated appeals" for over $4 billion worth of relief and rehabilitation assistance to more than 20 million people in some 20 countries—a rise of 29 percent from mid-1992. As relief activities climbed to claim two-thirds of the World Food

Programme's 1993 budget, the agency's resources available for development shrank accordingly. Similarly, U.S. migration and refugee assistance funds grew from $420 million in 1990 to $720 million in 1994, and the European Union's humanitarian aid tripled in just two years to about $700 million in 1993.[10]

Events in Rwanda provide a recent and particularly depressing example of the international community's shortsightedness. When the genocidal killings in that country began in early April 1994, the U.N. Security Council responded by reducing the peacekeeping force deployed there to a symbolic presence. In late April, Secretary-General Boutros-Ghali proposed boosting the force to 5,500, at a six-month cost of $115 million. Opposition by the Clinton administration delayed formal approval of the force, and the lack of adequate offers of troops and equipment from other governments postponed its deployment for months. By July, estimates of the number of people killed had risen to half a million. Hundreds of thousands more fled into neighboring Zaire following the victory of the Rwandan rebel army; cholera and dysentery epidemics ravaged the refugee camps. Only then did the outside world begin to act, by organizing a massive humanitarian relief effort. On July 22, 1994, Boutros-Ghali estimated that $435 million would be needed over six months (a figure later increased to $552 million). One week later, President Clinton announced that U.S. aid alone was surging toward half a billion dollars.[11]

It is far cheaper to try to avoid violent conflict than to cope with its repercussions— massive outpourings of refugees and humanitarian emergencies.

This points to a bitter irony. Presumably, concern about financial costs was one of the motivating factors, along with the perceived political costs, for blocking early deployment of a peacekeeping force that could have averted some of the bloodshed and prevented the exodus of civilians. But because resolute action was not taken, hundreds of thousands of lives were sacrificed and the costs to the rest of the world end up being incomparably higher. Furthermore, because of indecisiveness in working to reconstitute the political and legal institutions of this shattered country, its future stability remains in question.[12]

Piecing Together the Peace Puzzle

The U.S. Arms Control and Disarmament Agency and the Stockholm International Peace Research Institute both publish annual reports containing country-by-country military expenditure data. Yet, the reader looks in vain for comparable information on disarmament expenditures. In fact, it appears that no organization, inside or outside of government, is compiling any such data. This paper, then, represents the first systematic attempt to provide a picture of global peace and demilitarization expenditures in the post-Cold War era. Compiling such data is like trying to assemble a jigsaw puzzle with an unknown number of pieces and only a vague sketch of what the final picture will look like.

The paucity of information is no accident. It is a reflection of underlying perceptions and priorities. The category of military spending per se is well established and accepted, even though many governments keep secret at least some portions of their total defense spending. By comparison, government accounts contain no such thing as a disarmament budget proper. Virtually every sovereign state has its defense ministry, but only a few have a disarmament ministry.[13]

Locating peace and demilitarization expenditures in national budgets is tedious and difficult, requiring a familiarity with the different structures and idiosyncracies of each bureaucracy. Expenditures of this kind are often scattered across a number of ministerial budgets, including defense, foreign affairs, foreign aid, finance, energy, and trade and industry. Even within the same ministry, several different divisions or sections may be involved. Though there may be good reasons for this high degree of compartmentalization, the inherent fragmentation is likely to be detrimental to establishing disarmament as a strategic goal.

In some cases, separate units or agencies have been established—and their own budget line items created—to carry out newly arising arms control and disarmament tasks. For instance, a number of governments have formed treaty-verification units within their defense ministries. The U.S. Army set up a Chemical Materiel Destruction Agency to get rid of chemical weapons. The Dutch government, in its budget submission to Parliament, provides a single line for all arms control activities.[14]

But at least as commonly, such activities and expenditures are subsumed under already existing programs and budget titles, often those of military bureaucracies. The consequences are three-fold. First, disarmament is regarded as just another military task, perhaps of only temporary duration, rather than a significant change in the armed forces' basic mission. One British Ministry of Defence official was frank enough to describe the elimination of surplus tanks—by explosive charge—as actually providing the soldiers involved with some realistic training for their trade.[15]

Second, it is not always possible to tell what portion of a budget is devoted to disarmament purposes and what to traditional military endeavors. For example, the Spanish government combines its expenditures to destroy old battle tanks with those used to purchase new tanks. Likewise, the U.S. Department of Energy does not separate its costs to dismantle nuclear warheads from other costs at its weapons facilities.[16]

Third, disarmament-related expenditures are not fully reported. For example, governments typically employ regular armed forces personnel to dismantle weapons that are in excess of limits established by the Conventional Forces in Europe Treaty. In most cases, the salaries of those personnel are not incorporated into disarmament cost estimates because they would be paid anyway, even in the absence of any disarmament measures. Similarly, the use of satellite reconnaissance for treaty-verification purposes may not be considered attributable to disarmament, since the satellites would be in use even in the absence of arms control.[17]

As difficult as it is to track down national data, it can be mind-boggling to try to figure out peace and disarmament-related expenditures of international organizations, such as the United

Nations, the World Bank, the European Union, and the Organization of American States. Though most of them operate on the basis of regular annual or biennial budgets replenished by assessed contributions from member states, some of their activities are funded through voluntary contributions. Most have no budgets dedicated specifically or exclusively to demilitarization endeavors. Instead, such funding tends to be done on an ad hoc basis, with money coming from different budget lines, and sometimes becoming available only by the reallocation of undisbursed funds initially targeted for other purposes. The variety of funding arrangements and mechanisms can be bewildering, particularly when a multiplicity of donors, implementing agents, and beneficiaries is involved. Information about funding is typically fragmented, and data may be incomplete and sometimes even contradictory, making tracking exceedingly difficult.[18]

The expenditure data used throughout this paper are derived from a wide variety of sources, including published materials and private communications with officials at government agencies and embassies, international organizations, and experts at universities and public policy organizations. Within this array of sources, the availability of data varies considerably. And its quality is inevitably uneven, ranging from precise annual expenditures or appropriations, to back-of-an-envelope calculations, to rough-order-of-magnitude estimates, to—in some cases—no data at all. Certain governments are reluctant to make data available to the public—some requests for information simply went unanswered, and the French government, for example, considers its arms control budget classified. And some governments may not even know how much they are spending.[19]

Coping with the Legacy of War

A number of long-standing conflicts have been settled in recent years or are in the process of being settled—in Nicaragua, El Salvador, Ethiopia/Eritrea, Mozambique, Namibia, South Africa, Israel/Palestine, Lebanon, and Cambodia. As elating as this must be to the people in those countries, the transition from war to peace presents a host of new challenges.

War damage must be repaired or replaced, and vast areas littered with land mines await clearance. A representative political system, with an independent judiciary and strong democratic institutions, must be established and fair elections held to create political legitimacy and diminish the likelihood of a return to violence. War-shattered economies need to be revitalized to prevent economic discontent from undermining peace accords, refugees and displaced people repatriated and helped to restart life at home, and ex-combatants demobilized and reintegrated into civilian life. Many of these tasks are interrelated and therefore need to be tackled as a whole.

If successful, the reintegration of ex-combatants into civilian society not only reduces the long-term drain on scarce public budgets but also holds the promise of making the former fighters productive members of society. On the other hand, long delays in the demobilization process or the absence of opportunities for viable civilian careers following demobilization can have severe consequences. Ex-soldiers might either resort to criminal behavior for lack of some means of sustenance (as has happened in several countries) or regroup as a discontented fighting force, posing a serious danger to peace and stability.[20]

Given the exhausted economies of countries emerging from warfare, a significant share of the costs of demobilization and reintegration falls upon foreign donors.

Ideally, following the signing of a peace agreement, the combatants are brought to locations where they are registered, disarmed, and prepared to re-enter civilian society. During this so-called cantonment period (or, if possible, earlier), assessments are made of the ex-combatants' skills, needs and preferences, and of where they want to live. This information is crucial to designing well-tailored, effective reintegration programs. To smooth reintegration, such programs involve assistance targeted toward both short- and long-term needs, including cash compensation, provision of agricultural land and tools, housing, extension of credits, training and apprenticeship courses, and income-generating programs for former fighters and their kin.[21]

The challenge is enormous: in several countries, "Decades of war have produced one or two generations of functional illiterates, people who know how to shoot automatic weapons and set land mines, but who are not capable of tilling the...soil...or reading instructions to operate a well that could provide water for an entire community," as Francisco José Aguilar Urbina of the Arias Foundation in Costa Rica has commented. Many former soldiers therefore require substantial assistance.[22]

Very often, reality is far from the ideal just described. Among the factors that play a role in determining the outcome of demobilization programs are the political will to abide by commitments made under peace agreements; comprehensive, advance planning for what can be a lengthy and complex process; flexibility and resilience to cope with setbacks; and adequate coordination among the diverse actors involved—the previously warring parties, donors, international organizations, and non-governmental groups. Some or all of these ingredients may be in short supply.

In addition, no amount of good will and planning can make up for inadequate funding. As a 1993 World Bank report of seven country case studies points out, insufficient resources can cause delays in implementation, and hence lengthy encampment periods, and may at a later stage undermine effective support programs, such as promises of land and credit for ex-combatants and their families. These difficulties can lead to a loss of confidence in the whole process, produce an uneasy and tenuous peace, and might even make it unravel.[23]

The experience in certain countries has not been encouraging. In Afghanistan, Angola, Liberia, and Cambodia, demobilization was attempted but never fully implemented, and fighting has resumed. In Nicaragua and El Salvador, demobilization did take place, but reintegration has proved difficult; peace has been fragile. Efforts in Zimbabwe and Namibia were successful in the sense that a return to conflict was avoided, but there, too, reintegration has been problematic. (In Zimbabwe, the armed forces remained larger than initially planned, and the transfer of many ex-soldiers bloated the country's civil service.) The process remains to be completed in Uganda and Chad. In Mozambique, demobilization of government and rebel soldiers was completed more or less on schedule, but the formation of a smaller, unified army has been agonizingly slow.[24]

TABLE 3
Costs of Demobilization Programs, Selected Countries[1]

	Cost	Duration	Number Demobilized
	($ millions)		
Angola[2]	125.0	1992-93	19,833
Chad	18.9	1992-93	9,173
Mozambique	54.4-62.6	1993-94	77,000-83,000
Namibia	46.4	1989	32,000
Nicaragua[3]	84.4	1990-92	96,000
Uganda	19.4	1992-94	30,000 proj.
Zimbabwe[4]	230.0	1981-85	75,000

[1]It is difficult to directly compare costs in different countries because the data for some include items not reflected for others. [2]Demobilization was aborted; some 19,883 combatants had been demobilized before full-scale fighting resumed. [3]$43.6 million for Contra demobilization; $40.8 million for Sandinista Army demobilization. It is unclear how much was actually spent on Sandinista demobilization; assistance and benefits were promised, but the government received only $5.8 million in aid from Spain and, due to limited domestic funds, was unable to follow through on its promise. [4]Includes cost of combatants' salaries while they were encamped for one year or more ($42 million); such costs are not included in other cases here.

Sources: Adapted from World Bank, *Demobilization and Reintegration of Military Personnel in Africa: The Evidence from Seven Country Case Studies,* Discussion Paper, Africa Regional Series, Report No. IDP-130 (Washington, D.C.; October 1993); Humberto Ortega Saavedra, "The Role of International Financial Institutions in the Democratization and Demilitarization Process," in Francisco José Aguilar Urbina, ed., *Demobilization, Demilitarization, and Democratization in Central America* (San José, Costa Rica: Arias Foundation for Peace and Human Progress, Centre for Peace and Reconciliation, 1994).

Given the exhausted state of the economies of countries emerging from warfare, the costs of demobilization and reintegration (see Table 3) are often beyond the nations' capacity. Hence, a significant share of financing falls upon foreign donors. However, though the early availability of resources is critical to designing adequate programs, donors have been reluctant to make such commitments. They often prefer to wait until they detect signs of a successful program, yet that very delay reduces the likelihood of success. Without knowing how much aid they can expect during what period of time, the governments of countries return-

ing to peace cannot adequately plan or launch a demobilization program.[25]

Efforts to remove land mines are another key ingredient in
the success of post-conflict reconstruction. Scattered indis-
criminately, land mines have become a ubiquitous threat and a
powerful impediment to the normal functioning of a society,
even long after a war has ended. Most mines are found in rural
areas, and many of the countries most afflicted by them depend
predominantly on agriculture for income and employment.
Without effective demining programs, large areas of land remain
inaccessible, refugees are impeded or discouraged from return-
ing home, peasants cannot work their fields, and reconstruction
is hindered. And coping with the needs of mine-blast survivors
can easily overwhelm a poor country's health and social systems.

The statistics are chilling. Of approximately 1 million persons
who have been killed or maimed by land mines since 1975, some
80 percent were civilians. Every month, mines cause more than
800 deaths or injuries. Estimates of the number of mines scattered
in some 62 countries range from 65 million to more than 100 million (see Table 4), or one mine for every 50 to 85 people on earth.
In the 12 countries with an "extremely severe" problem (as judged
by the U.S. State Department), there is one mine for every three
to five people. And the mines continue to be laid far faster than
they are being removed: each year, even as clearing operations
struggle to remove roughly 80,000 mines, perhaps as many as 2
million new ones are being laid. More than 250 million land
mines have been produced over the past 25 years, and production
runs from 10 to 30 million each year; an additional 100 million
mines are thought to have been stockpiled.[26]

Mine clearance is not only extremely dangerous—under-
taken "one leg, one life at a time," as some commentators have
put it—but also very time-consuming and expensive. Experience
suggests that it takes 100 times as long to detect, remove, and dis-
arm a mine as to plant it. Mines are extremely cheap to man-
ufacture, but according to Patrick Blagden, the United Nations'
top de-mining expert, it could cost an astronomical $200-300 bil-
lion to clear all mines worldwide. Just removing mines newly
laid in an average year could take at least $600 million.[27]

TABLE 4

Estimated Number of Uncleared Mines, by Region and Selected Country

Countries Affected (by region), and Total Number of Mines	Worst-Affected Countries	Number of Mines
		(millions of mines)
Africa		
18 countries	Angola	9
18-30 million mines	Mozambique	2
	Somalia	1-1.5
	Sudan	0.5-2
	Ethiopia/Eritrea	0.3-1
Middle East		
At least 8 countries	Iraq	5-10
17-24 million	Kuwait	5-7
East Asia		
8 countries	Cambodia	4-7
15-23 million		
South Asia		
At least 5 countries	Afghanistan	9-10
13-25 million		
Europe		
13 countries	Bosnia, Croatia, Serbia	2.5-3.7
3-7 million		
Latin America		
8 countries	Nicaragua	0.1
0.3-1 million	El Salvador	0.02

Source: Adapted from Human Rights Watch/Arms Project and Physicians for Human Rights, Landmines: A Deadly Legacy (New York, et al.: Human Rights.

Nothing like this large amount of money is available. Kuwait, which signed de-mining contracts worth about $700 million after the Iraqi occupation, is spending far more than the rest of the world combined. Elsewhere, de-mining efforts—when undertaken at all—tend to be badly underfunded. In a number of countries with ongoing U.N. peacekeeping operations, voluntary trust funds have been set up to finance mine clearing, but Secretary-General Boutros-Ghali has said that "This system is usually slow and inadequate to meet the need for urgent mine-clearance programs." Some $25 million per year has been spent on de-mining efforts in the context of peacekeeping operations in Mozambique, Somalia, Cambodia, and Afghanistan in recent years, a figure expected to rise to $28 million in 1995. Altogether, all U.N. agencies spent some $67 million on mine clearance and mine awareness during 1993. In Central America, the government of El Salvador and the Organization of American States spent a total of $8 million in 1993 and 1994.[28]

The International Red Cross has estimated it could take thousands of years to clear all mines in Afghanistan. De-mining there is now concentrated on just 60 square kilometers of priority areas, but shortfalls in funding have impeded even that limited effort. Likewise, removing all mines in Cambodia clearly surpasses that impoverished country's capacity; it would require every Cambodian to contribute every dollar of income for several years. Human Rights Watch and the Physicians for Human Rights have called on the countries that stoked the fires of the Cambodian conflict to provide funding and other assistance for mine clearance. In Mozambique, the U.N. mine-clearing program proceeded so slowly that the Dutch government decided to withdraw its contribution from the trust fund set up for the purpose.[29]

There is not only insufficient money to undertake urgently needed demining, to increase mine awareness among civilians, and to provide anything near adequate care for survivors of mine explosions, but also little prospect of any technical breakthroughs that might help make mine clearing less life-threatening. Armed forces have developed techniques to breach mine fields, but these are unsuitable for making mined areas habitable again. A coalition of groups calling for a ban on land mines is making remarkable progress toward stigmatizing these "hidden killers." Several governments have declared moratoria on exporting mines, but some still seem more interested in refining mine technologies (developing supposedly "self-destructing" mines, for instance) than in pursuing a comprehensive production ban. For example, even though the German government has joined a voluntary moratorium on mine exports, its 1994 budget nevertheless contains 355 million deutsche marks (DM)—some $230 million—for R&D and procurement of land mines.[30]

Land mines have become a ubiquitous threat and a powerful impediment to the normal functioning of a society, even long after a war has ended.

Effective mine clearance must be done before refugees can return to their homes. The number of international refugees has grown tenfold, from 2.4 million people in 1974 to about 23 million in 1994. In addition, there are an estimated 26 million "internally displaced" people—those who felt compelled to abandon their homes but did not flee across an international border. All in all, one out of every 114 people in the world has been uprooted by conflict. Wherever conditions allow, refugees do eventually return home, many with the assistance of the U.N. High Commissioner for Refugees (UNHCR) and other agencies. In 1992, a record 2.4 million refugees were repatriated, equivalent to 13 percent of the refugee population that year. UNHCR was planning to help 3 million people go home during 1994—in countries such as Guatemala, Mozambique, Rwanda, and Sri Lanka. But with new conflicts breaking out across the globe, the returnees' numbers are dwarfed by legions of newly displaced people. Returnees notwithstanding, during the last two decades the total number of refugees grew in every single year except two.[31]

Although most UNHCR funds go to accommodate refugees in their new host countries, a rapidly growing amount of money is devoted to voluntary repatriation—rising from $43 million in 1988 to $207 million in 1993 and a projected $382 million in 1994. Repatriating refugees can be more than twice as expensive as keeping them in camps. UNHCR provides returnees with the basics for a new start in their homeland: tools, seeds, building materials, and sufficient food before the first harvest.

The agency also tries to provide or repair infrastructure such as water wells, roads and bridges, and schools and health clinics. But as UNHCR official Soren Jessen-Petersen explains, "We are not able to rebuild entire countries, and there really aren't any international agencies which are. There is a real gap in the international system here."[32]

The financing required to secure the success of war-to-peace transitions in countries like El Salvador, Nicaragua, Cambodia, and Mozambique is quite small compared to global aid flows, and certainly small in contrast to the resources that for many years were devoted to sustaining wars. Still, for the countries involved, weakened by protracted conflict, they are quite substantial. (See Table 5.) Timely and adequate support from the international community is crucial to firming up what otherwise might be a shaky or temporary peace. Yet, as Oscar Arias Sánchez, former Costa Rican President and 1987 Nobel Peace Prize Laureate, pointed out in the Central American context, "Each day the hope that our countries will receive as much aid for human development as they once received for militarization grows increasingly remote."[33]

By and large, bilateral donors and international organizations such as the World Bank, the U.N. Development Programme (UNDP), and the European Union are just beginning to come to grips with the requirements and implications of war-to-peace transitions. For them, demobilization and reintegration are still emerging issues; with ad hoc arrangements predominating, many donors are institutionally not geared up for timely and effective support.[34]

There are exceptions, though. UNDP has been involved in a small number of innovative projects linking post-conflict rehabilitation, peacebuilding, and long-term sustainable development. The projects—in Central America, Cambodia, Sudan, and Afghanistan—aim in particular to alleviate poverty, which is often the root condition of conflict. They are designed and implemented with strong participation by the intended beneficiaries.[35]

UNDP's Central American experience, according to officials, has the potential to serve as a model that could be applied to other regions emerging from long years of warfare. Two projects— CIREFCA (the International Conference on Central American

Refugees) and PRODERE (the Program for Displaced Persons, Refugees and Returnees)—helped 210,000 refugees return home and extended credits and other assistance to 470,000 persons to rebuild war-destroyed communities. PRODERE concentrated on 40 war-scarred municipalities characterized by widespread poverty. It adopted a strong local focus in its efforts to rehabilitate or create health and education systems and economic development agencies, and it put particular emphasis on the protection of rights and the strengthening of public participation in decision-making. The project also marked the first time ever that UNDP and a number of other U.N. agencies "operated together under a joint work plan with a common budget."[36]

CIREFCA and PRODERE funds—a total of $438 million was mobilized between 1989 and 1994—came primarily from European countries. PRODERE has spent approximately $20 per beneficiary per year. By contrast, Guatemala and Honduras spent that much for military purposes per capita of their entire populations each year during the 1980s; in El Salvador and Nicaragua, the military absorbed $40-90 per capita.[37]

The roles of the World Bank, the International Monetary Fund (IMF), and the regional lending institutions in particular need to be rethought. The World Bank is receiving an increasing number of requests for technical and financial aid for ex-combatant reintegration, and it has assisted Angola, Ethiopia, and Uganda. However, the Bank's involvement has so far been reluctant and relatively minor.[38]

The overall lending policies of the World Bank (and the IMF) are likely to have a more significant impact than the Bank's limited direct involvement. And that impact may be detrimental. The so-called "structural adjustment" conditions that both institutions routinely insist on as a prerequisite for approving loans may actually be at odds with the goals of post-conflict reconstruction. First, by putting strict limits on the recipient governments' public spending, these provisions by implication also restrict outlays to help foster peace and reconciliation. Second, by imposing cutbacks in social programs that alleviate poverty and prescribing export-oriented economic policies, these arrangements tend to accentuate domestic inequalities and may generate

TABLE 5
Financing Post-Conflict Reconstruction[1]

Country	Observation
Guatemala	The government and the URNG guerrilla force were expected to sign a formal peace agreement by late 1994 to end 30 years of conflict. The government created a "National Fund for Peace" (FONAPAZ) in 1991 to finance refugee resettlement and social and economic rehabilitation in the poorest regions affected by the conflict. With international support, FONAPAZ investments rose from $6.3 million in 1992 to $13 million in 1993 and a projected $34 million in 1994.
El Salvador	International donors pledged $800 million for peace accord's implementation and reconstruction (including demobilization and reintegration of 42,000 ex-combatants, elections, democratization and safeguarding human rights, and redistribution of land), but far less money has been forthcoming. Some $515 million of national and international funds are available for 1993-96, leaving a shortfall of at least $376 million.
Haiti	Emergency Economic Recovery Program, to be implemented in the 6 to 12 months following a return to democracy, will cost about $210 million. Foreign donors have pledged more than $1 billion for social and economic rehabilitation over five years.
Mozambique	Implementation of peace agreement—including electoral aspects—is estimated to cost close to $100 million just in 1994. Refugee repatriation, demobilization and reintegration of ex-combatants, and mine clearance will cost at least $150 million more. Rebuilding destroyed schools, and humanitarian needs require many hundreds of millions of dollars.
South Africa	Development Bank of Southern Africa calculated the cost to overcome the consequences of apartheid in areas such as health, education, employment, social services, and infrastructure—and hence to create conditions under which a peaceful multi-racial society can be viable—at $16 billion in capital investments and annual expenditures of $9 billion for several years. DBSA assumes the country's economic base will permit such investments only stretched out

TABLE 5 (CONTINUED)

	over a decade, even with strong economic growth. The African National Congress has developed an $11 billion, five-year reconstruction and development plan that remains as yet in draft form.
Palestine	In 1993, donors pledged $2.4 billion over five years to lay an economic foundation for Palestinian self-rule in Gaza and Jericho. However, relatively little money has been forthcoming ($200 million by November 1994), threatening the viability of self-rule. The U.N. Relief Works Agency, meanwhile, launched a Peace Implementation Programme with $173 million worth of projects.
Kuwait	Kuwait spent at least $8-10 billion on reconstruction contracts with foreign companies during 1991-93 following the Gulf War (including $1 billion to fight hundreds of oil-well fires set by the departing Iraqi army). Cost estimates made immediately following the war were in the $20-25 billion range over five years. The government has not released any official figures, but submitted a $41-billion claim against Iraq for damages inflicted.
Cambodia	Of $880 million pledged by foreign donors for reconstruction and peacebuilding in June 1992, only about $200 million had actually been disbursed by September 1993 when the new elected government was formed.
Bosnia	The cost of restoring essential public services in war-devastated Sarajevo is estimated at $540 million, with $254 million needed urgently and $286 million for a transitional phase.

[1] The term "reconstruction" is broadly used here to encompass a variety of post-conflict activities, including repair of physical damage, demobilization and rein-tegration of ex-combatants, resettlement of refugees and displaced persons, and creation of the social, economic, and political conditions under which peace can take root. The presence and importance of each one of these varies from case to case.

Sources: See endnote 33.

new discontent that could bear the seeds of future conflict. As Liisa North, a professor at York University, Canada, has pointed out, the austerity measures imposed today on many countries emerging from conflict contrast sharply with the generous aid that some European and Asian countries received following World War II.[39]

El Salvador and other countries emerging from war are likely to find themselves walking a tightrope between the contradictory demands of fulfilling loan conditions on the one hand and peace accords on the other. In 1990, Anthony Lake, now President Clinton's National Security Advisor, warned that "Economic policies that exacerbate...instability may destroy the peace completely." He elaborated, "Concern for the survival of fragile democratic institutions and achievement of the political stability needed to preserve a newly won peace suggests that the World Bank and IMF should be particularly careful about the policies upon which they insist as a condition of their participation in the reconstruction of...war-torn regions."[40]

Thinning Out the Arsenals

The late 1980s and early 1990s witnessed a series of unprecedented arms control and disarmament treaties on conventional, chemical, and nuclear arsenals. Of these, however, only one—the Chemical Weapons Convention—is global in scope. The two Strategic Arms Reduction Treaties (START I and II) concern only the United States and the former Soviet Union; the Conventional Forces in Europe Treaty, as its name suggests, regulates armaments only on that continent. The Third World is largely outside the framework of these new treaties.

The chemical treaty is also the only one that mandates the destruction of stockpiles and production facilities. The others represent no more than a thinning out of huge existing arsenals. Still, these agreements, together with cuts in military spending and reductions in armed forces and military bases, represent a significant break with past trends and policies. The companies, workforces, and communities that used to depend on military largesse face both a challenge—adjusting to this new reality—and an opportunity—reorienting themselves toward civilian endeavors.

In signing the START I and II treaties, the United States and the Soviet Union (for START II, it was Russia) committed themselves to ending the relentless buildup of nuclear weapons. (The signatories began to take steps consistent with the treaties even prior to their coming into force.) Fulfilling the treaty commitments will require decommissioning or destroying large numbers of ballistic missiles and missile silos, strategic bombers, and submarines; this further implies dismantlement of thousands of warheads, and storage or disposal of huge quantities of fissile materials and rocket fuels. The costs of these measures will be substantial, but will be more than offset by future savings. In any event, they pale in comparison with the roughly $5 trillion (in 1993 dollars) that these countries have spent since 1946 to acquire and maintain their arsenals. And substantial savings are in the offing. Compared with spending plans prior to START I and II, the U.S. Congressional Budget Office estimated that the United States could save more than $20 billion per year by taking steps not necessarily mandated by, but consistent with, START.[41]

Countries emerging from war are likely to find themselves walking a tightrope between the contradictory demands of fulfilling loan conditions on the one hand and peace accords on the other.

The Pentagon's full estimate of its START-related costs remains classified, but some of the larger components can be identified. The U.S. Navy has so far spent more than $700 million to dismantle ballistic missile submarines, and the Air Force projects spending $130 million to reduce strategic bombers and land-based missiles and to destroy missile silos. These disarmament costs are quite moderate when compared to ongoing armaments programs. The Air Force, for example, has initiated a 10-year program to prepare and equip its 95 B-1B nuclear bombers for conventional missions, at a cost of $2.5 billion. It is spending an additional $4.6 billion to extend the operational life of its Minuteman-III missiles and improve their accuracy.[42]

The U.S. Department of Energy has been dismantling between 1,000 and 1,600 nuclear warheads annually in recent years. The Office of Technology Assessment has estimated annual dismantlement costs to be $500 million to $1 billion over the next decade. Following warhead disassembly, the surplus plutonium will most likely be placed in storage for several years, at an estimated cost of $2 to 3 billion for a decade. Because the ultimate fate of the plutonium and highly enriched uranium contained in the warheads is uncertain, final disposition costs for these materials are unknown (though they are likely to range from a few hundred million to several billion dollars).[43]

Unclassified assessments by the Russian military estimate that implementing START would cost Russia 90 to 95 billion rubles. Expressed in 1992 prices, this would be equivalent to about $6 billion, though the ravages of Russian inflation render any dollar estimates somewhat arbitrary. The other former Soviet republics with nuclear arms have agreed to ship them to Russia for dismantlement. Strapped for funds, Ukraine has asked for international assistance of up to $2.8 billion to accomplish this, and Kazakh President Nursultan Nazarbeyev has asked for $1 billion in compensation to rid his country of nuclear weapons.[44]

The other declared nuclear powers—China, France, and the United Kingdom—are not part of any nuclear arms control agreements. To the extent that they dismantle any warheads, it is principally for routine maintenance and overhaul. In its 1994 budget, the French government, for example, revealed for the first time how much it spends on disassembling nuclear warheads. The sum, about 65 million francs ($11 million), is tiny compared with the roughly $4 billion that France devoted to its nuclear weapons program during the same year.[45]

The international convention outlawing the possession of chemical weapons and mandating the destruction of existing stocks is expected to enter into force during 1995. A new body, the Organization for the Prohibition of Chemical Weapons, is being set up to carry out inspections to ensure global treaty compliance. Initial plans foresaw a staff of up to 1,000 and an annual budget in the range of $150 to 180 million, but Western nations, focused on cost-cutting, insisted on a much smaller staff (now expected to number some 365). At $29.7 million, the budget approved for 1994 is roughly half of the amount requested. For 1995, the budget could rise to $60-75 million, and once the OPCW is fully operational, annual inspection costs may come to $75-100 million. The head of the OPCW's Provisional Technical Secretariat, Ian Kenyon, has already lamented the intense workload of his staff. Some outside observers have pointed out that the smaller staff size and circumscribed resources may eventually compel the OPCW to dispatch smaller inspector teams for shorter lengths of time than originally planned, possibly compromising its ability to detect, and hence deter, treaty violations.[46]

Unclassified assessments by the Russian military estimate that implementing START would cost Russia $6 billion.

Complying with the Chemical Weapons Convention will be very costly for the United States and Russia, the only countries that have acknowledged possession of such weapons: destroying chemical weapons is reckoned to cost up to 10 times as much as producing them. Russian President Boris Yeltsin said in 1993 that destroying his country's stocks could cost more than all of Russia's other disarmament programs combined.[47]

The program to incinerate the U.S. stockpile has experienced large cost overruns; estimates now run to $9.6 billion (plus an additional $17.7 billion to properly dispose of old, buried chemical ammunition). Annual funding for the U.S. Army's Chemical Materiel Destruction Agency has risen from less than $200 million in the late 1980s to more than $500 million.[48]

While the United States has begun to destroy small amounts of chemical weapons, Russia's program has been delayed by technical difficulties, lack of money, and popular opposition; destruction is to begin by 1997. It is next to impossible to come up with any reliable cost projections. The U.S. experience does not offer much of a benchmark for comparative purposes. Although Russia may end up relying on U.S. technology, its cost structure is very different; and although Russia has more weapons than the United States, unit-per-unit they should be less costly to destroy because they do not contain explosive charges. Official Russian cost estimates have varied widely; in mid-1994, a Russian diplomat put the cost at $1.3-2.8 billion. Russia hopes that 30-40 percent of the cost will be covered by foreign assistance and the sale of chemical byproducts salvaged from the weapons stocks.[49]

The Conventional Forces in Europe (CFE) Treaty sets national limits for major pieces of military equipment (such as tanks and combat aircraft) deployed between the Atlantic and the Urals. It came into force in 1992 and is to be fully implemented by November 1995. The treaty gives signatories a number of options to get rid of excess equipment, including export to other countries, so that only a portion of the surplus items is actually being dismantled.

Among members of the North Atlantic Treaty Organization (NATO), Germany and the United States have by far the largest expenses in carrying out the CFE Treaty's provisions. Germany faces a large task because it needs to dispose of the equipment of the former East Germany. It spent 1.5 billion DM—about $900 million—in 1991-94 on CFE (and on other arms control activities). The United States spent $134 million, but other signatories' annual costs are typically less than $5 million or so.[50]

The former Warsaw Pact states have to undertake far larger reductions in their arsenals than NATO members, but they also have very limited resources for this task. Though their expenditures may not seem particularly large by Western standards— the Czech Republic had spent $2 million by early 1994, and Belarus estimates its total cost at $33 million—they are substantial for these economically hard-pressed countries. During a 1994 meeting of the Joint Consultative Committee (a body created to oversee implementation of CFE), these countries unsuccessfully called for the creation of an international fund to support weapons destruction. Russia has repeatedly complained about its CFE costs. To meet the treaty's zonal sub-limits, Moscow needs to shift troops and equipment and therefore build new bases and housing. Russia would prefer, in effect, to let its surplus weapons rust away rather than undertake the expensive process of cutting them apart.[51]

The CFE Treaty does not regulate ammunition stocks, but many countries are reducing their holdings anyway. The global market to dispose of explosives and restore contaminated sites could grow from more than $1 billion in 1993 to $7 billion by 2000. The United States, Russia, Belarus, Ukraine, and Germany are among those countries with the largest surplus. The U.S. Army demilitarized about 300,000 tons of ammunition during 1990-95, at a cost of about $300 million. That is only about as much money as the Army requested for 1994 and 1995 to preserve the capacity to manufacture ammunition in the future. And 1990-94 Congressional appropriations to procure new ammunition add up to a staggering $6.6 billion.[52]

> **Russia would prefer to let its surplus weapons rust away rather than undertake the expensive process of cutting them apart.**

Overall, the United States, Russia, and Germany are incurring by far the largest disarmament-related expenses. For Germany and particularly for the United States (see Table 6), a fair amount of reliable information is available. The opposite is true for Russia: available data are minimal, and where figures do exist, they are rendered almost meaningless by severe economic and political uncertainties. For example, some 837 billion rubles were allocated for disarmament purposes in the 1994 budget, but since Parliament didn't approve the budget until May 1994, actual expenditures may bear little relation to the published budget figures.[53]

Adjusting to the Drawdown

Conversion—the process of transferring skills, equipment, and other resources from the military to the civilian realm—is imperative for any serious demilitarization policy to succeed.

Internationally, it is an important confidence-building measure, to the extent that it helps make disarmament less reversible. Domestically, it can help reduce the pressure for continued high levels of arms production and export and/or maintaining obsolete military bases, by smoothing the impact of reduced military spending on companies, employees, and communities.

This impact has become increasingly felt since the mid- to late 1980s, when worldwide employment in the arms industry peaked at approximately 16 million. During the remainder of that decade, a quarter million of these jobs were cut, and at least 3-4 million additional jobs are expected to be lost by 1998. Similarly, of approximately 32 million soldiers worldwide in 1990, some 2.2 million were demobilized in 1990-92, with a roughly equal number still to be cut. As large numbers of military facilities are closed in the former Soviet Union, North America, and Europe, substantial numbers of civilians employed by the armed forces will lose their jobs as well.[54]

The base-closure process differs markedly between East and West. Particularly in the United States, it is a highly structured and planned process that includes environmental assessments and economic adjustment programs. In Russia, the process matches the country's turbulent economic situation; lacking adequate resources, bases are apparently being closed in anything but an orderly fashion. In most countries, there is insufficient information on the costs and benefits associated with base closures. Some governments do not collect the requisite data, others are just beginning to embark on closures, and still others did not respond to queries.[55]

Even in the absence of precise data, it seems safe to assume that the savings realized from not operating these bases will likely offset the closure cost within a few years at the most. (In some cases, the costs could be substantial due to the need to clean up soil and water contamination.) Although closing a base causes economic ripple effects in the local economy, civilian reuse eventually provides more jobs and greater economic opportunity than the military presence did, particularly if the reuse is well planned.

The United States is in the middle of a wave of base closures initiated in the late 1980s. Closures decided upon in 1988,

TABLE 6

U.S. Arms Control and Disarmament Expenditures, 1989-94

	1989	1990	1991	1992	1993	1994
	(million dollars)					
ACDA[1]	32	34	37	45	47	54
OSIA[1]	39	29	79	86	69	87
INF Treaty[1]	128	78	84	86	[40]	[40]
START Treaty[1]	17	39	59	141	277	220
CFE Treaty[1]	0	0	0	51	26	22
Chemical Weapons[2]	180	270	316	421	583	610
Ammunition Disposal	17	15	31	50	35	68
Nuclear Verification and Control Technology[3]	155	166	196	229	325	362
Base Closure	0	538	998	1,148	2,120	2,765
Conversion/Economic Adjustment	0	0	200	1,000	1,260	2,150
Total[4]	568	1,169	2,000	3,257	4,782	6,378

[1]The activities of the Arms Control and Disarmament Agency (ACDA) and the On-Site Inspection Agency (OSIA) relate to implementation of existing arms control agreements; the expenditures listed for the INF, START, and CFE treaties and for Chemical Weapons are those of government agencies other than ACDA and OSIA. [2]Activities to carry out Congressionally mandated destruction of U.S. chemical weapons stockpile and to prepare for implementation of the Chemical Weapons Convention and the U.S.-Soviet Chemical Weapons Agreement. [3]Conducted by the Department of Energy. [4]Not included are Department of Energy expenditures for nuclear warhead dismantling, for which no precise annual figures are available; the Office of Technology Assessment has estimated that these costs are likely to be in the range of $500 million to $1 billion per year.

Source: See endnote 53.

1991, and 1993 will cut about 15 percent of the domestic base infrastructure; the last round of closures, in 1995, could involve as many facilities as the first three combined. The total costs to implement all closure decisions are estimated at nearly $15 billion during 1990-99, of which $4 billion is for environmental cleanup. But the projected savings in operating funds over the same period of time would more than offset the expenditures. Additional costs and savings are being incurred as the Pentagon closes some 895 overseas military installations and returns home some 174,000 troops.[56]

Although the term conversion has entered the lexicon of decision-makers, actual conversion policies remain rare. Governments are forced to prune their military industries, but they are intent on protecting, not dismantling, their "defense industrial base." The adjustment to lower military spending is largely left to the market, resulting in mergers, plant closures, and job loss. In an overview of strategies pursued around the world, Herbert Wulf of the Bonn International Center for Conversion rated conversion efforts in Europe, the United States, Russia, and the developing world as "small or unimportant."[57]

In the United States, prior to the Clinton administration, very limited federal funding was earmarked for conversion efforts. President Clinton proposed making available close to $20 billion during 1994-97 under his Defense Reinvestment and Conversion Program. But this figure is less impressive than it appears to be.[58]

First, more than one-third of this amount is funding under a variety of high-tech initiatives that may well offer civilian alternatives to arms industry firms but is not targeted per se toward their conversion. Second, another 30 percent is money devoted to so-called "dual use" projects, aimed ostensibly at developing technologies with either civilian or military application. But the military mission remains key to these programs, some of which are simply repackaged military R&D projects. Conversion is "not what we're about," commented Lee Buchanan, director of the Technology Reinvestment Project (TRP), the core of the dual-use program. Dorothy Robyn of the National Economic Council confirmed that TRP "is aimed at preserving defense capabilities." Only about one-third of the dual-use funds are civilian-oriented, according to Greg Bischak, executive director of the National Commission for Economic Conversion and Disarmament in Washington, D.C. Adjusting the Clinton budget accordingly yields a less spectacular $8.5 billion for true conversion.[59]

Besides the amount of funding, at least two other problems arise. The first concerns the distribution of beneficiaries: while two-thirds of the allotted money would go to companies, only one-third is devoted to assisting their workforces and defense-dependent communities. The second concerns the implementing agency: the Pentagon is to be in charge of disbursing a large share of the funds, even though it has proven itself reluctant to promote any serious switch from military to civilian purposes. In fact, when the first adjustment funds were provided in fiscal year 1991 legislation, the Pentagon raised several objections and delayed release of the funds for 10 months.[60]

In Europe, conversion funding by central governments is marginal or nonexistent.

In Europe, conversion funding by central governments is marginal or nonexistent. The little money available seems mostly bound up in efforts to restructure defense industries and safeguard their survival, not bring about their reorientation. Regional and local governments are struggling to fill the void, but frequently lack adequate resources. Among the continent's largest military powers and arms producers, Britain, Germany, and Spain have not created any national conversion budgets at all. The Italian government's 1994 budget contains a conversion appropriation of about 500 billion lire (some $320 million), but it is dwarfed by a $2.4 billion package to recapitalize the state-owned military industry firms. The French Ministry of Defense created a Fund for Defense Restructuring in 1991, to provide investment aid for small and medium-sized firms hit hard by military procurement cuts. Its impact, however, is limited by its small size—240 million francs (about $45 million). A larger fund, the Accompagnement Structurel des Industries de Défense (ASTRID), was created in 1993, with a capital endowment of about 700 million francs ($125 million).[61]

The two Germanys were among the most militarized countries on earth; now unified Germany faces one of the largest tasks among European countries in adjusting to a shrinking military.

As in neighboring countries, reduced military procurement has increased the pressure on the arms industry, already faced with substantial overcapacities, to downsize. But in addition, the army of East Germany was dissolved, ex-Soviet troops completed their withdrawal in August 1994, and a large portion of the NATO troops stationed in western Germany were pulled out. According to Herbert Wulf, of the more than 2.1 million military-related jobs in 1990, less than half are likely to remain once the retrenchment is completed.[62]

For the German economy as a whole, the adjustment does not pose any insurmountable challenge. Yet individual regions, such as the state of Brandenburg (which was host to half of all Soviet bases in East Germany) or Rheinland-Pfalz (where close to 10 percent of all employment was military-related in the 1980s) are more vulnerable. The federal government initially promised to set up a special 1 billion DM ($600 million) support fund and in 1991 entered negotiations with the states over the level of federal financial aid. But after it took measures to increase the flow of tax revenues to the states, the government argued that the states ought be able to shoulder the costs of disarmament and conversion without further federal assistance. Though state revenues remain insufficient, the federal government rejected all appeals for establishing a conversion budget. (It provided only some 131 million DM, or about $79 million, out of the military budget to compensate eastern German companies whose military procurement contracts were cancelled in 1990.)[63]

For regions and communities struggling to move away from their economic dependence on military spending, the European Union's PERIFRA and KONVER programs are an alternative to national aid programs. They were created to assist with job retraining, regional diversification through new enterprises, support for business innovation, and cleanup and reuse of military bases. To be eligible for grants, national, state, or local governments applying for assistance have to provide matching funds, in effect doubling the funding available. Funding came to a relatively modest 90 million European Currency Units (a little over $100 million) in 1991-92, but for 1994-98, a budget of

500 million ECUs (about $570 million) has been proposed.[64]

In the Third World, conversion is much less an issue—few countries possess sizable arms industries, and those that do are more likely to build up than to decrease their capacities. A handful of countries—including Argentina, Brazil, Israel, and South Africa—are exceptions. In place of explicit conversion strategies, however, the military industries of these countries are undergoing a downsizing process. In Argentina, this is part of a World Bank-supported privatization policy; in Brazil, a number of companies have gone bankrupt.

China is switching a large part of its arms industries to producing civilian goods, but using proceeds to modernize arms production.

The Israeli government has provided subsidies to aid the restructuring process and to support laid-off workers. The Philippines provides an example of base-conversion efforts. The country inherited huge military facilities when the U.S. military departed; Subic Bay naval facility was closed in 1992. Subic Bay Metropolitan Authority was subsequently established to put the former base to commercial use by attracting foreign investors.[65]

China has pursued its own brand of conversion, switching a large part of its arms industries to producing civilian goods, but using at least part of the proceeds to finance investments to modernize arms production. From the late 1970s to 1990, the government allocated more than 3 billion yuan to conversion and modernization of industrial production capacities. During 1991-95, a total of 6 billion yuan (some $1.14 billion at 1991 exchange rates) is to be invested. China also began demobilizing large numbers of troops in the late 1970s. The estimated costs (particularly officers' pensions) have been substantial, ranging from $2 billion to $5 billion or more annually in recent years.[66]

When Eastern Europe moved out of the Soviet orbit, the new leadership regarded conversion as an attractive political and economic proposition. Arms production collapsed after 1989, and defense industries in the region went into "hibernation," as Judit

Kiss, a Hungarian-born analyst, put it. Limited funds went to stabilize the heavily indebted arms industry and to help develop civilian production. But conversion became a dirty word when the West not only failed to provide assistance to weather the difficult transition but also went after the markets once catered to by East European arms producers. Mindful of resurgent nationalism in the region, and suspicious of Russian intentions, governments tried to protect the core of their industries, with an eye to reconstructing a smaller, more modern arms industry.[67]

From the late 1980s, the Soviet and then Russian government kept drawing up ambitious conversion plans that were never implemented. Thanks to drastically lower domestic weapons procurement and collapsing arms exports, the Russian military industry is in a state of disintegration. Military equipment production has declined by 78 percent since 1991. The industry did increase the volume of its civilian output, but successful conversion was prevented by political upheaval and the chaotic transition from a centrally directed to a more market-oriented economy. Estimates in 1992 put the total costs of conversion at $150 billion, far surpassing Russia's financial capacities.[68]

Russian government budgets do include an annual allocation for conversion—some 1 trillion rubles (about $980 million) in 1993, and 755 billion rubles (less than $500 million) in 1994. Yet, according to Julian Cooper, director of the Centre for Russian and East European Studies at the University of Birmingham, the published figures are almost meaningless. First, rapid inflation erodes budgetary purchasing power, necessitating budget revisions during the same fiscal year. Second, since 1992, planned allocations have been disbursed only partially and after long delays. Information about actual spending is unreliable. Third, the bulk of the sums being disbursed—perhaps as much as 80 percent—goes not to retooling military factories but to subsidizing workers' salaries in order to prevent social unrest. In addition to budgetary grants, the Russian state makes conversion credits available at preferential interest rates, and local governments' budgets have become an important source of conversion financing. But information on these funds, too, is unreliable. Cooper concludes that "It is impossible to construct anything

remotely resembling a meaningful data set" on Russian conversion spending.[69]

With few conversion successes and the specter of large-scale
military industry layoffs, Russia has moved from conversion
euphoria to an anti-conversion backlash. There are indications
that the government is becoming more interested in boosting the
industry's exports than in switching it to civilian production.[70]

"Pulling the Fangs Out of the Bear"?

Given the dramatic political and economic dislocations in the
former Soviet Union, the successor states are confronted
with an enormous challenge in meeting their disarmament
obligations—one they may not master without foreign help. A
number of Western countries have agreed to provide assistance
to dismantle nuclear warheads, to safely transport and store the
fissile materials contained in them, to convert arms factories, and
to construct housing for soldiers previously stationed abroad.

Between 1990 and 1994, the Soviet Union, and then Russia,
withdrew more than 700,000 soldiers and 500,000 civilian dependents from Central and Eastern Europe and from other countries—the largest peacetime military
pullout in history. But the returnees
are confronted with problems such
as a severe housing shortage and a
lack of civilian skills. Russian Defense
Minister Pavel Grachev claimed in
1993 that the number of officers
without proper housing would rise
from 120,000 in early 1993 to
400,000 in 1994. Grants and credits
made available by Germany to facil-
itate the pullout of ex-Soviet troops from the former East
Germany add up to 12.6 billion DM ($7.6 billion) in 1991-95,
including 7.8 billion DM for housing construction and 200 million DM for civilian training of officers. (Other countries' assistance in this regard is almost insignificant by comparison.)[71]

Grants and credits made available by Germany to facilitate the pullout of ex-Soviet troops add up to $7.6 billion.

Western assistance in other areas is much less generous. Russian aid requests of $1 billion for its struggling chemical weapons destruction efforts sharply contrast with roughly $60 million worth of aid pledged by the United States and Germany. France, Germany, Italy, Japan, and the United Kingdom combined have so far offered some $200 million worth of nuclear-disarmament-related assistance stretched over several years, with additional, larger aid pledges from the United States.[72]

Under what is known as the Nunn-Lugar program, the U.S. Congress has given $400 million in each fiscal year since 1992 to the Pentagon to assist Russia, Belarus, Ukraine, and Kazakhstan—principally for nuclear disarmament, with limited funds going to chemical disarmament and conversion. Putting these funds to use—negotiating umbrella and implementing agreements—has proven to be an agonizingly slow process, in part because of bureaucratic and political impediments in the Soviet successor states. Of $1.2 billion appropriated in 1992-94, budget authority for $212 million expired before proper agreements were signed. Although the Pentagon managed to conclude agreements that committed virtually all of the remaining funds, it expected actual obligations—and hence spending—to reach no more than $420 million by the end of fiscal year 1994.[73]

In addition to the Nunn-Lugar funds, the United States will purchase 500 tons of highly enriched uranium derived from Russian nuclear warheads over the next 20 years—to be diluted and used as fuel for civilian nuclear power plants. Initially, the sale may bring Russia some $240 million annually, rising later to $725 million per year. The entire deal is worth about $11.9 billion.[74]

Another area of Western assistance concerns defense conversion, but the funds made available to date are trivial. The Organisation for Economic Co-operation and Development maintains a register that appears to be the most comprehensive list of actual and planned projects involving Western donors. For 1991-94, they add up to a paltry $200 million (though preliminary 1994 data understate the level of funding).[75]

The European Bank for Reconstruction and Development (EBRD) has a mandate that explicitly involves conversion, but its efforts to date have been very limited. Its criteria for conversion lending in effect render the bulk of the former Soviet arms producers ineligible for support. In 1992, the EBRD began to initiate a number of "diagnostic" studies of Russian military enterprises and to develop about 20 projects that might receive some funding; the majority of these, however, are in the exploratory stage, and actual funding to date has been low by the EBRD's own admission.[76]

Out of 1.87 billion ECUs (about $2.2 billion) made available in 1991-94 under the European Union's TACIS Program (Technical Assistance to the Commonwealth of Independent States), only a tiny portion—34.5 million ECUs ($40 million)—has been devoted to conversion. The U.S. government is allocating similarly small amounts of money, hoping that it will be a catalyst for much larger amounts of private capital. In a report to Congress, Secretary of Defense William Perry admitted that U.S. conversion assistance "is a very small fraction of what is actually needed...."[77]

In addition to involving limited funds, U.S. and European programs have another unfortunate commonality: much of the money is being spent in the donor countries on feasibility studies and fees, travel, and office expenses for Western consultants—75 percent in the U.S. case, leaving little for actual retooling and retraining in Russia or other former Soviet republics. Moreover, some Western-sponsored "conversion" projects have managed to stir resentment among the intended beneficiaries, including one that paired NPO Mashinostroyenia, a high-tech military design bureau in Russia, with a cola-bottling U.S. firm. Russian suspicion is growing that the United States may be less interested in projects that advance conversion and disarmament in East and West than simply "to pull the fangs out of the Soviet bear," as Senator Richard Lugar, co-sponsor of the Nunn-Lugar program, has said.[78]

Building Institutions for Peace

Peace and demilitarization tasks are being handled in a largely improvisational manner. A number of intergovernmental consultative committees have been set up in the framework of arms control treaties (along with corresponding national implementing agencies), but in many other areas discussed in this paper, there are no specifically dedicated international organizations or structures.

To put a peace system on a more reliable foundation, it may be useful to transform what now are often ad hoc activities into more permanent ones. This step might include the creation of a disarmament verification agency, a satellite monitoring unit, permanent peacekeeping and conflict-mediation capacities, a sanctions council and support fund, an electoral observation agency, and an international criminal court (along with a strengthened World Court).

To create confidence that far-reaching disarmament enhances rather than undermines security, effective inspection and monitoring arrangements are needed. A few countries now have pools of experienced verification personnel, and the International Atomic Energy Agency (IAEA) has for many years been running a safeguards program to prevent the use of nuclear technology for weapons purposes. However, many other countries do not have any inspection capabilities, or lack the resources to create them. The IAEA, meanwhile, suffers from severe shortcomings: it failed to detect Iraq's nuclear weapons program, and because it is also tasked with the promotion of civilian nuclear energy, its effectiveness is compromised. As non-proliferation becomes a key security concern, the international community has a growing need to be able to distinguish civilian from military uses of technologies that could serve either purpose. Given the global interconnections of research and development, production, investment, and trade, the verification challenge is inherently global.

A new International Verification Agency might be charged with inspection responsibilities for nuclear, chemical, and conventional disarmament. It could build upon, and eventually incorporate, the Organization for the Prohibition of Chemical Weapons that is currently being set up in The Hague, Netherlands, to verify global adherence to the Chemical Weapons Convention. A new agency could also draw upon the experience gained by the U.N. Special Commission that, since 1991, has shared responsibility with the IAEA for detecting and eliminating Iraq's weapons of mass destruction.

The capabilities of the verification agency could be augmented by a Satellite Monitoring Agency. Additional tasks that might be accomplished with the help of such an agency include conflict prevention, peacekeeping, confidence-building measures, and economic sanctions. Satellite-based detection would help warn against surprise attacks, confirm or refute alleged border violations, and detect any illicit flows of weapons or embargoed wares.

Peacekeeping operations are a key component of an alternative security policy. They have grown dramatically in number, size, and complexity, encompassing such tasks as monitoring cease-fires, disarming combatants, repatriating refugees, and monitoring elections. Expenditures have grown from about $250 million in the late 1980s to $3.7 billion in 1994. But these missions have run into considerable difficulties. One handicap is that they are still being established and financed on an ad hoc basis. It is time to establish a permanent peacekeeping force and supporting infrastructure, financed by a regular annual budget. In addition,

A new International Verification Agency might be charged with inspection responsibilities for nuclear, chemical, and conventional disarmament.

to avoid having peacekeeping forces become little more than a global fire brigade, it would be useful to establish a conflict early-warning capability and standing conflict-resolution committees in different regions of the world.[79]

Economic sanctions can play an important role in conflict resolution, although it is clear that they cannot produce peace on their own. They have long been used unilaterally by individual nations, but are now, after the Cold War, increasingly resorted to by the international community. Specific committees have been set up by the U.N. Security Council to oversee each of the embargoes it imposed in recent years. However, in order to enhance their effectiveness and systematize them as part of an overall peace policy, it may be useful to establish a sanctions council within the U.N. framework.[80]

In addition, a support fund could assist countries that, due to their economic reliance on the target country, find it difficult to bear the burden of complying with international sanctions. Examples include Macedonia (vis-à-vis Serbia), Jordan and Turkey (vis-à-vis Iraq), and, until recently, the Dominican Republic (vis-à-vis Haiti). Macedonia's sanctions-related economic losses, for instance, have been put by the U.N. at $2 billion just up to the end of 1993. A group of more than 50 developing countries has been pushing for the fund's creation, but Western nations opposed the idea, preferring that the International Monetary Fund and the World Bank address the issue. In 1993, a U.N. General Assembly Working Group reached an impasse over the proposal for a voluntary fund for such purposes.[81]

Elections are frequently part of national peace and reconciliation accords. Though no panacea, assuring fair elections and acceptance of the outcome is a crucial ingredient of efforts to avoid a return to civil war (or, in polarized societies, a slide toward violence). International electoral assistance and monitoring missions play an important role in this process. In recent years, the U.N., regional organizations, and several non-governmental organizations have become increasingly involved in such activities. By mid-1994, there had been election-related U.N. missions in almost 50 countries, some of them in conjunction with peacekeeping operations. In order of rising complexity, duration, and cost, they entailed technical assistance (the most common involvement), coordination of international monitors, verification, supervision, and—so far in only one case, Cambodia—the actual organization and conduct of elections.[82]

In response to rising requests, an Election Assistance Unit was formed in early 1992 in the U.N. Department of Political Affairs; it has since been upgraded to a Division. But its financial means—a voluntary trust fund—seem insufficient to meet the rising demand. And much of the assistance rendered still has an ad hoc character; there is a lack of internationally accepted norms and rules for the proper conduct of both elections and electoral assistance and monitoring. The Swedish government in 1992 initiated a commission to evaluate the feasibility of an International Electoral Institute that could help with these questions, and perform other tasks such as studying past experiences, maintaining a databank on available personnel and resources, conducting training programs, and professionalizing electoral assistance.[83]

An indispensable part of a new peace policy relates to the strengthening of international law. The International Court of Justice in The Hague, popularly known as the World Court, has been in existence for half a century. But it has never been used to its full capability in resolving international disputes, because national governments have shied away from referring cases to it, or have refused to be bound by the Court's judgment. If the routine settlement of disputes by non-violent means is to become a reality, most or all nations wil have to submit to the Court's mandatory jurisdiction. This would imply a considerable strengthening of the Court, which now has a limited staff and an insignificant budget of about $9 million per year.[84]

In addition to the World Court, there have long been proposals to establish an International Criminal Court that would have jurisdiction over cases of aggression, genocide, and other crimes against humanity, and serious violations of international humanitarian law during armed conflicts. (Perhaps operating alongside it would be a global investigative body to produce evidence for cases to be tried before that court—a possibility mentioned in 1994 congressional testimony by U.S. Secretary of State Warren Christopher.)[85]

International tribunals were established by the U.N. Security Council in 1993 to prosecute war crimes committed in the former Yugoslavia and in 1994 to investigate the genocide in Rwanda. However, these efforts appear to suffer from insufficient financial and political support by the international community.[86]

Although the idea of creating an international court that could try accused perpetrators of war crimes is not new—it arose out of the Nuremberg trials of the leaders of Nazi Germany—it is now receiving more serious consideration in the United Nations, the United States, and the European Union. The Geneva-based International Law Commission, established by the U.N. General Assembly in 1947 to help develop and codify international law, has been at work on the issue since 1989. A draft statute for an international court was submitted in 1993 to U.N. members for their comments; a revised version was to be submitted to the General Assembly in late 1994. With the Assembly's consent, preparatory meetings and a treaty negotiating conference could occur during 1995 and 1996.[87]

How much might these initiatives cost? Of course, that depends on the tasks to be accomplished. Concerning a verification agency, for instance, crucial cost variables include the number of facilities to be inspected, the type and frequency of inspections, the number of people required, and the specialized equipment and skills they may need. In addition, any arms treaty that, like the Chemical Weapons Convention, outlaws production altogether rather than limiting it, makes the verification task easier. On the other hand, if prohibited weapons activities share characteristics with permitted civilian activities (chemical weapons precursor substances, for example, are legitimate materials in the civilian chemical industry), verification poses a greater challenge and the costs are likely to be greater as well. The costs of a verification agency may well run to several hundred million dollars per year.[88]

In the early 1980s, the U.N. commissioned a group of experts to study the implications of establishing an international satellite monitoring agency. The group estimated the equipment and operating costs to be perhaps $800-900 million per average year. Including costs for staff, facilities, and overhead, the average annual cost, expressed in today's dollars, would likely be about $1 billion.[89]

The establishment of a permanent peacekeeping force, including proper decision-making and logistics infrastructures, would imply costs above current expenditures. But it would also save money by avoiding the inefficiencies of current ad hoc efforts. Permanent structure or not, better training is important to improving peacekeeping operations. A study by the Washington, D.C.-based Henry Stimson Center estimates that staff and operating costs of a center able to train 1,500 persons per year would cost about $21 million annually. The estimate does not include the facility itself; however, with large numbers of military bases closing down, governments could make one or several sites available and conceivably donate them to the U.N.[90]

Though creating institutions such as those discussed in this section is likely to involve billions of dollars per year, the costs are not very large when compared with military expenditures. The truly significant obstacle is of a different nature: many governments lack the political will to create an alternative security system. Until that will materializes—and sufficient pressure is brought to bear on decision-makers—these institutions will not be established even if they cost little. In place of a deliberate strategy to create such entitites, it is more likely that the current ad hoc efforts will be expanded wherever and whenever the circumstances of the day demand it.

Establishment of a permanent peacekeeping force would save money by avoiding the inefficiencies of current ad hoc efforts.

A Global Demilitarization Fund

Since the end of the Cold War in 1989, governmental spending on peace and demilitarization has increased rapidly. According to Worldwatch Institute estimates, governments and international organizations have spent roughly $50 billion for these purposes between 1989 and 1994. Demilitarization expenditures have increased five-fold, but still represent only 1 percent of the amount devoted to the military during that period. Since the database on which this estimate is based contains certain gaps, total spending is somewhat higher—by at least several hundred million dollars and possibly a few billion dollars a year. In particular, our estimate under-reports expenditures associated with base closures and some of those relating to disarmament (especially concerning the former Soviet Union). And it does not include post-conflict reconstruction, because of inconsistent and partial data.

As suggested throughout this paper, the world does not spend nearly enough on peacebuilding and demilitarization. Demining efforts are badly underfunded. Postwar reconstruction suffers from a lack of donor generosity and foresight. Peacekeeping is in a chronic state of financial crisis. Expenditures to implement arms control treaties appear roughly sufficient in Western nations, but not in former Warsaw Pact countries strapped for resources. Most countries are determined to spend as little as possible on treaty compliance and verification. And arms conversion needs are neglected by almost all governments.

Much of the spending is aimed at coping with the military legacy and at cutting the fat out of military arsenals. By contrast, next to nothing goes to efforts to help bring about a future less reliant on military prowess: institutions capable of enforcing and verifying restrictions on arms production and shipments, and forums that provide early conflict warning, peaceful settlement of disputes, and reconciliation services.

Aside from the amounts of money involved, an important question concerns to what extent they are mandatory, discretionary, or voluntary. Mandatory expenditures are those required as part of membership in international organizations (such as assessments for U.N. peacekeeping), or by certain multilateral agreements (such as assessments for the new Organization for the Prohibition of Chemical Weapons). Voluntary expenditures include contributions to the U.N. High Commissioner for Refugees, to the array of U.N. trust funds (set up for purposes such as election monitoring, demobilization and reintegration of ex-combatants, and land-mine clearance), and to humanitarian relief operations. Discretionary expenditures are those incurred in implementing international treaties that mandate certain activities such as reductions in tanks or nuclear missiles but that do not prescribe any particular level of spending to guarantee compliance. Most peace and demilitarization expenditures are discretionary or voluntary rather than mandatory.

Many governments have been less than exemplary in paying dues obligated by international law (for example, during 1994,

TABLE 7

Global Peace and Demilitarization Expenditures, 1989-94[1]

Category	1989	1990	1991	1992	1993	1994
			(million dollars)			
Demining	10	10	197	200	238	241
Demobilization	46	28	38	54	56	52
Refugee Repatriation	77	101	160	172	252	463
Disarmament						
Nuclear	1,174	1,214	1,706	1,775	2,007	1,998
Conventional	25	26	144	351	321	529
Chemical	180	270	317	421	591	586
Aid to Former USSR	0	0	1,275	1,708	2,370	1,984
Other	126	124	199	218	206	246
Base Closures	na	538	998	1,148	2,120	2,864
Conversion	93	114	511	1,302	1,609	2,707
Peacekeeping/-building	749	677	760	2,149	3,450	4,080
World Court/War Crimes						
Tribunal	6	9	9	9	9	20
Total	2,486	3,111	6,314	9,507	13,229	15,770

[1]This table represents the first systematic attempt to compile global peace and demilitarization expenditures. The data come from a wide variety of sources with differing degrees of reliability. Thus they are a composite of precise expenditure figures, annual averages of multi-year figures, and estimates. In some cases, data were inconsistent; in other cases, none were available. Occasionally, the distinctions among the expenditure categories are blurred: peacekeeping operations, for example, now frequently encompass such activities as demining, demobilization, and refugee repatriation, but it is difficult or impossible to determine what part of an operation's budget covers these. Similarly, some conversion spending might be attributed to the base closures category.

Source: Worldwatch database.

U.N. members owed the organization close to $2 billion for peacekeeping). But non-mandatory contributions carry even more uncertainty. Under voluntary arrangements, funding is vulnerable to governments' changing priorities and the political pressures of the day, with substantial year-to-year fluctuations the likely result. The shaky nature of funding for peace is mirrored in the ad hoc quality of many demilitarization endeavors; on such a basis, it is impossible to build the foundations for a more peaceful world.[91]

There is, in short, a need for reliable, permanent institutions and an International Fund to facilitate such endeavors. This is what former Costa Rican President and 1987 Nobel Peace Prize Laureate Oscar Arias Sánchez proposed recently. The proposal developed here follows Arias' arguments, but is somewhat broader in scope.[92]

The Fund would serve three fundamental purposes and therefore would have three distinct components. The first is to assist countries that lack adequate resources for coping with the legacy of war. This "restitution account" would provide financial support for such endeavors as demining, armed forces demobilization and reintegration, refugee repatriation, and post-conflict reconstruction.

The second component would provide the financial underpinning for weapons dismantlement and economic conversion efforts that reach far beyond contemporary measures. This "transformation account" is predicated on the adoption of international accords that mandate deep reductions or even the elimination of deployed weapons systems, and establish meaningful barriers against future production, possession, trading, and use of arms.

The third component is to provide resources for building an effective, alternative global peace system. This "peacebuilding account" would help transform what are now ad hoc activities into more reliable and permanent ones. It would assist the establishment of new international institutions and mechanisms for disarmament verification, peacekeeping, conflict mediation and settlement, election monitoring, and other purposes.

Where would the Fund resources come from? The most obvious source is military budgets. Transferring money from these accounts to such a Fund would help capture at least a portion of the elusive peace dividend. A conceptually elegant step suggested by Arias would be to earmark each year a predetermined share of the money saved from reductions in the military budget of each nation. The savings would be measured against the military expenditures in a given base year. As long as cuts continue to be made in military spending, the savings relative to the base year would accumulate, and the Fund contributions would therefore grow each year. But the annual contributions would stay unchanged if military budget cuts ceased, and they would decline if military expenditures increased. The magnitude of Fund resources would be chronically unpredictable. Countries not reducing or perhaps increasing their spending would in effect be rewarded, those undertaking cuts punished. The endeavor might come to be regarded as a "tax" on disarming, when the activity that should be "taxed" is arming.

A dual formula could counter these weaknesses—with the base tier being a percentage of the military budget and the second tier being a share of the reductions in military spending. The Fund would be less vulnerable to short-term fluctuations, because if the revenue base of one tier declined, that of the other would increase. Assuming that participation in the Fund eventually became mandatory, a dual formula would also ensure that all countries contribute to it, even though some may choose not to cut their own military spending.

Initially, acceptance of "the principle of committing a portion of the peace dividend to promoting global demilitarization," as Arias puts it, is most important; contributions could at first be made voluntary. But eventually, the Fund needs to play more than a symbolic role; contributions could then be made a normal requirement of a country's U.N. membership, just like payments to the organization's regular and peacekeeping budgets.[93]

How much funding could be expected under the proposed formula? Arias proposes that industrial countries set aside one-fifth of their peace dividend for the Fund, and developing countries one-tenth. The *Human Development Report 1994*'s figures for global military spending, and its assumption that military expenditures will drop by 3 percent annually for the rest of this decade, provide the basis for a rough calculation. Using 1994 as the base year, Arias' formula would yield about $85 billion during 1995-2000, an average of $14 billion per year. (Obviously, the outcome would vary tremendously, depending on which year was selected as the base year. Choosing 1990 instead of 1994 would yield $225 billion over the same period.) If base-tier contributions were pegged to a value of 1 percent of global military expenditures, that would yield an additional $42 billion during 1995-2000, or close to $7 billion per year. Total revenues would thus reach $126 billion. (See Table 8.)[94]

Criteria for deciding who is eligible to receive assistance under the restitution and transformation accounts would have to be developed. Two kinds of judgments would be needed: whether a country is unable to marshal sufficient domestic resources and therefore *needs* assistance, and whether that country is committed to demilitarization and therefore *deserves* assistance. Any country receiving Fund assistance would have to provide some matching funds. Any country applying for Fund assistance would be expected to submit relevant data to the U.N.'s Standardized Reporting System on Military Expenditures and to the U.N. Register of Conventional Arms Transfers.

Promoting greater openness concerning national military expenditures (and establishing criteria for what items are to be considered part of military spending) would be crucial for calculating Fund contributions. Although some governments are fairly open about their military budgets, and some have submitted data to the U.N., it would currently be very easy for most governments to evade paying their fair share of the Fund simply by continuing to conceal portions of their spending. Resolving the openness issue poses substantial political problems, however, because it confronts deeply ingrained notions of secrecy in the name of national security.

The issue of who would administer the Fund is another delicate one. Developing countries could be expected to prefer a U.N. General Assembly-like setup—that is, the one-country, one-vote principle. Yet this arrangement would make most Western governments reluctant to commit to the Fund, for lack of control over it. They can be expected to favor a solution akin to that of the World Bank or the IMF—that is, the largest contributors make the decisions. Another issue concerns whether the Fund should be a separate entity or be made part of an existing organization. Clearly, the details of implementation are

TABLE 8
Hypothetical Contributions to a Global Demilitarization Fund, 1995-2000

	1995	1996	1997	1998	1999	2000	1995-2000
	(billion dollars)						

First-tier contributions: 1% of global military expenditures:

	1995	1996	1997	1998	1999	2000	1995-2000
Military Expenditures	744	722	700	679	659	639	4,143
Fund Contributions	**7.4**	**7.2**	**7.0**	**6.8**	**6.6**	**6.4**	**41.4**

Second-tier contributions: 20% of savings in military expenditures, relative to 1994 base year,[1] for industrial countries, 10% for developing countries:

1. Industrialized Countries:

	1995	1996	1997	1998	1999	2000	1995-2000
Military Expenditures	630	611	593	575	558	541	3,508
Savings	19	38	56	74	91	108	386
Fund Contributions	**3.8**	**7.6**	**11.2**	**14.8**	**18.2**	**21.6**	**77.2**

2. Developing Countries:

	1995	1996	1997	1998	1999	2000	1995-2000
Military Expenditures	114	111	107	104	101	98	635
Savings	4	7	11	14	17	20	73
Fund Contributions	**0.4**	**0.7**	**1.1**	**1.4**	**1.7**	**2.0**	**7.3**

	1995	1996	1997	1998	1999	2000	1995-2000
TOTAL FUND CONTRIBUTIONS	**11.6**	**15.5**	**19.3**	**23.0**	**26.5**	**30.0**	**125.9**

[1]1994 base year: Military expenditures of industrial countries = $649 billion; expenditures of developing countries = $118 billion; world total = $767 billion.

Source: Worldwatch calculation based on projected military expenditures and cumulative military budget savings in Table 3.1. of United Nations Development Programme, *Human Development Report* 1994 (New York and Oxford: Oxford University Press, 1994).

vital to determining whether governments would be prepared to support the establishment of such a Fund.

Because Western governments would shoulder the bulk of Fund contributions, their attitude is decisive. Their track record in development aid—most have failed to meet the international goal of providing 0.7 percent of their GNP—is not reassuring, and they currently have little appetite for creating what they may regard as just another bureaucracy. Although their leaders like to talk about moral and humanitarian values, altruism is unlikely to carry the day. They cannot be expected to support a disarmament fund unless they perceive that their relatively narrow self-interests would be served by it. In this context, at least three arguments can be made.[95]

First, as the Rwanda episode has demonstrated, conflict prevention is infinitely cheaper than continuation of the status quo—not an insignificant fact in the cost-conscious 1990s. And a permanent structure would save money, just by avoiding the duplications and other inefficiencies inherent in today's ad hoc demobilization, peacekeeping, and humanitarian relief activities. Second, in an era of ever-expanding global trade and investment, countries at war or unstable because of unresolved disputes are in effect "lost markets" to traders and investors. And third, the societal breakdown that is typically associated with domestic conflicts today unleashes growing waves of refugees. It is as obvious as it is regrettable that Western countries are already reaching their limits of tolerance toward admitting more people seeking political asylum. Establishing and funding effective peacekeeping and peacemaking institutions would provide benefits in all three areas.

Establishing a demilitarization fund would require the same sense of mission and destiny that motivated the founders of the United Nations and the Bretton Woods institutions following World War II. Given today's political constraints, such a fund is, realistically, a long-term prospect. But transitional measures are conceivable. U.N. peacekeeping operations, for example, already encompass an enormous variety of tasks, including demining, demobilization, and refugee repatriation. Most of the non-military, peacebuilding components of these operations, however, are being financed through voluntary contributions. Funding them through regular, assessed contributions levied on all U.N. members—in effect having a reliable funding mechanism for many of the activities described in this paper—is one modest step that could easily be taken now.[96]

To reap the benefits of peace, governments need to shed their penny-wise, pound-foolish stance. If peace is considered unaffordable, it will remain elusive. At a time when politicians' strategic thinking rarely extends beyond the next election campaign, it will take courageous leadership to launch visionary initiatives now that will yield peace dividends for generations to come.

Notes

1. Michael Oreskes, "Poll finds U.S. Expects Peace Dividend," *New York Times*, January 25, 1990, and John Zarocostas, "UN: Peace Dividend Could Free $35 Billion a Year for Development," *Journal of Commerce*, May 23, 1991.

2. United Nations Development Programme, *Human Development Report 1994* (New York and Oxford: Oxford University Press, 1994).

3. Development of global military spending from UNDP, op. cit. note 2, and from Michael Renner, "Military Expenditures Falling," in Lester R. Brown, Christopher Flavin, and Hal Kane, *Vital Signs 1992* (New York and London: W.W. Norton & Co., 1992). Herbert Wulf, "Conversion as an Investment: Costs and Benefits," paper prepared for the Monterey Institute of International Studies, May 1993.

4. Middle Eastern prospects from Julian Ozanne and Roger Matthews, "Ploughed Back Into Swords," *Financial Times*, September 9, 1994.

5. Number of major wars from Birger Heldt, Peter Wallensteen, and Kjell-Åke Nordquist, "Major Armed Conflicts in 1991," in Stockholm International Peace Research Institute (SIPRI), *SIPRI Yearbook 1992: World Armaments and Disarmament* (New York: Oxford University Press, 1992), and from Peter Wallensteen and Karin Axell, "Major Armed Conflicts," in SIPRI, *SIPRI Yearbook 1994* (New York: Oxford University Press, 1994). Trend of number of all wars from "Anzahl der pro Jahr geführten und der neu begonnenen Kriege," *Frieden 2000*, February 1993.

6. Discussing the costs associated with disarmament, arms conversion, and military cleanup, a prominent German peace researcher, Dr. Peter Lock, argued in 1992 that "the burden of our overmilitarized past will continue to present bills of possibly prohibitive dimensions." Peter Lock, "The Economic Costs of Peace — An Assessment of the Burden to Overcome the Burden of the Military-Bureaucratic-Industrial Complex," in Anke Brunn, Lutz Baehr, and Hans-Jürgen Karpe, eds., *Conversion — Opportunities for Development and Environment* (Berlin, Heidelberg, and New York: Springer Verlag, 1992).

7. Military-to-peacekeeping spending ratio from Michael Renner, "U.N. Peacekeeping Expands," in Lester R. Brown, Hal Kane, and David Malin Roodman, *Vital Signs 1994* (New York and London: W.W. Norton & Co., 1994). McCain quoted in *Washington Weekly Report. A Review of Congressional Action Affecting Multilateral Issues and Institutions* (Washington, D.C.: United Nations Association of the United States), Issue No. XX-19, June 28, 1994. Pentagon officials have voiced concerns similar to McCain's. See Eric Schmitt, "Pentagon Worries About Cost of Aid Missions," *New York Times*, August 5, 1994. Defeat of funding proposal from *Washington Weekly Report*, Issue No. XX-28, September 23, 1994.

8. UNDP, op. cit. note 2.

9. For a discussion of some of these issues and cost estimates, see Michael Renner, "Assessing the Military's War on the Environment," *State of the World 1991* (New York: W.W. Norton, 1991), and Michael Renner, "Cleaning Up After the Arms Race" *State of the World 1994* (New York: W.W. Norton, 1994).

Comprehensive analyses of the costs of war are rare. A notable exception is Michael Cranna, ed., *The True Cost of Conflict* (London: Earthscan, November 1994), a compilation of seven in-depth case studies examining human, economic, social, and environmental costs of conflict by Saferworld, a research organiza- tion in Bristol, United Kingdom.

10. UNHCR budget from Dutch Ministry of Foreign Affairs, *Humanitarian Aid Between Conflict and Development* (The Hague, November 1993). U.N. consoli- dated appeals from Boutros Boutros-Ghali, Secretary-General of the United Nations, *Report on the Work of the Organization from the Forty-Seventh to the Forty- Eighth Session of the General Assembly* (New York: United Nations, September 1993), and from U.N. Department of Humanitarian Affairs, "Secretary-General Reports to Economic and Social Council on Strengthening Coordination of Emergency Humanitarian Assistance," Briefing Note, New York, July 5, 1994. World Food Programme from United Nations, "Pledging Conference for Development Activities Begins Two-day Session," 1994 U.N. Pledging Conference for Development Activities, First Meeting, Press Release DEV/2038, CA/8786, November 1, 1994. U.S. funds from U.S. Congress, Foreign Operations, Export Financing, and Related Programs Appropriations Act, fiscal years 1990 to 1994. European Union from "ECHO Becomes Important Relief Fund," *D+C— Development and Cooperation*, No. 4, 1994.

11. Rwanda events from Paul Lewis, "U.S. Forces U.N. to Put Off Plan to Send 5,500 Troops to Rwanda," *New York Times*, May 17, 1994, from Michael R. Gordon, "U.N.'s Rwanda Deployment Slowed by Lack of Vehicles," *New York Times*, June 9, 1994, from Douglas Jehl, "Officials Told to Avoid Calling Rwanda Killings Genocide," *New York Times*, June 10, 1994, from U.N. Daily Highlights Press Release DH/1712, August 19, 1994, and from Milton Leitenberg, "Anatomy of a Massacre," (op-ed), *New York Times*, July 31, 1994. Projected peacekeeping force costs from United Nations, "Report of the Secretary-General on the Situation in Rwanda," S/1994/565, 13 May 1994. Boutros-Ghali's relief cost esti- mate from U.N. Press Release SG/SM/5375, IHA/528, "Secretary-General Addresses Opening of Inter-Agency Appeal in Aid of Persons Affected By Rwandese Crisis," July 22, 1994. Revised estimate from U.N. Security Council, "Progress Report of the Secretary-General on the United Nations Assistance Mission for Rwanda," S/1994/1133, October 6, 1994. Clinton estimate from White House, Office of the Press Secretary, "Statement by the President," Press Release, July 29, 1994.

12. Failure to assist reconstitution of government and national institutions from Donatella Lorch, "In Rwanda, Government Goes Hungry," *New York Times*, September 18, 1994, and from Raymond Bonner, "In Sea of Aid, Rwandans Lack Basics," *New York Times*, November 2, 1994.

13. New Zealand, for instance, has a Ministry for Disarmament and Arms Control. The last, post-Communist government of East Germany established a Ministry for Disarmament and Defense. But the government lasted only a few months before East Germany was absorbed into unified Germany—which has a traditional defense ministry but no counterpart for disarmament. A handful of small countries such as Costa Rica and Iceland have no armed forces and hence no military establishment, obviating any need for a disarmament ministry.

14. U.S. Army from Marilyn J. Tischbin, Chief, Public Affairs Office, U.S. Army Chemical Materiel Destruction Agency, Aberdeen Proving Ground, Maryland, private communication, January 24, 1994. Dutch situation from Robert Vester, Ministerie van Defensie, The Hague, private communication, July 26, 1994.

15. Wing Commander Mike Stokes, Ministry of Defence, United Kingdom, London, private communication, July 28, 1994.

16. Spanish situation from Vicenç Fisas Armengol, Centre UNESCO de Catalunya, Barcelona, Spain, private communication, July 14, 1994. U.S. Department of Energy from Office of Technology Assessment (OTA), *Dismantling the Bomb and Managing the Nuclear Materials* (Washington, D.C.: U.S. Government Printing Office, 1993).

17. Failure to include salary costs from Andrew S. Duncan, Assistant Director for Information, International Institute for Strategic Studies (IISS), London, private communication, December 14, 1993. One of the few countries to include salary costs is Germany. See *Bundeshaushaltsplan 1994, Einzelplan 14, Geschäftsbereich des Bundesministeriums der Verteidigung*, Kapitel 1409, "Rüstungskontrolle und Abrüstung," (Bonn, Germany: 1994). General Accounting Office (GAO), *Arms Control: Intermediate-Range Nuclear Forces Treaty Implementation*, GAO/NSIAD-91-262 (Gaithersburg, Maryland: September 1991); Congressional Budget Office (CBO), *U.S. Costs of Verification and Compliance Under Pending Arms Treaties* (Washington, D.C.: September 1990).

18. Author's general experience in data collection effort and private communications with Nat Colletta, World Bank, East Africa Department, Population and Human Resources Division, Washington, D.C., August 29, 1994, with Jennifer Tufts, Delegation of the European Commission, Washington, D.C., August 22, 1994, with Clemencia Muñoz, United Nations Development Programme, Regional Bureau for Latin America and the Caribbean, New York, September 1, 1994, and with Johanna Mendelsohn, U.S. Agency for International Development, Office of Transition Initiatives, Washington, D.C., August 15, 1994.

19. French situation from Duncan, op. cit. note 17.

20. Refugee Policy Group, "Challenges of Demobilization and Reintegration. A Discussion Paper," prepared for a working meeting sponsored by U.N. Department for Humanitarian Affairs and held in New York, June 7, 1994; Herbert Wulf, "The Demobilization of Military Personnel as a Problem and a Potential for Human Development," in Francisco José Aguilar Urbina, ed., *Demobilization, Demilitarization, and Democratization in Central America* (San José, Costa Rica: Arias Foundation for Peace and Human Progress, Centre for Peace and Reconciliation, 1994).

21. Refugee Policy Group, op. cit. note 20; World Bank, *Demobilization and Reintegration of Military Personnel in Africa: The Evidence from Seven Country Case Studies*, Discussion Paper, Africa Regional Series, Report No. IDP-130, October 1993.

22. Francisco José Aguilar Urbina, "Preface," in Aguilar Urbina, op. cit. note 20.

23. World Bank, op. cit. note 21.

24. Refugee Policy Group, op. cit. note 20; World Bank, op. cit. note 21; *International Security Digest*, June 1994; Nicole Ball, Director, Program on Enhancing Security and Development, Overseas Development Council, Washington, D.C., private communication, October 11, 1994; United Nations, "Third Progress Report of the Secretary-General on the United Nations Observer Mission in Liberia," S/1994/463, April 18, 1994; United Nations, "Sixth Progress Report of the Secretary-General on the United Nations Observer Mission in Liberia," Security Council Document S/1994/1006, August 26, 1994; Howard W. French, "As War Factions Shatter, Liberia Falls Into Chaos," *New York Times*, October 22, 1994; U.N. Daily Highlights Press Releases DH/1710, August 17, 1994 and DH/1715, August 24, 1994.

25. World Bank, op. cit. note 21.

26. Number of mine victims since 1975 from James P. Grant, Executive Director, U.N. Children's Fund, Statement before the U.S. Senate Appropriations Committee, Subcommittee on Foreign Operations, Hearing on the Global Landmine Crisis, Washington, D.C., May 13, 1994; percentage of civilian victims from Cyrus R. Vance and Herbert A. Okun, Statement before Landmine Hearing, op. cit. in this note; monthly casualties from U.N. General Assembly, "Moratorium on the Export of Anti-personnel Land-mines. Report of the Secretary-General," A/49/275, New York, July 27, 1994; number of mines scattered from Human Rights Watch/Arms Project and Physicians for Human Rights (HRW and PHR), *Landmines: A Deadly Legacy* (New York, et al.: Human Rights Watch, October 1993); mines-to-people ratio in countries with "extremely severe" situation is a Worldwatch calculation based on U.S. Department of State, *Hidden Killers: The Global Problem with Uncleared Landmines* (Washington, D.C.: Department of State, 1993), and on Population Reference Bureau, "1993 World Population Data Sheet," Washington, D.C., April 1993; production during past 25 years from Kenneth Anderson, Director, The Arms Project of Human Rights Watch, Landmine Hearing, op. cit. in this note; annual production estimate from United Nations, "UNHCR Calls for International Ban on Land-Mines," Press Release REF/1084, May 26, 1994.

27. HRW and PHR, op. cit. note 26; Donovan Webster, "One Leg, One Life at a Time," *New York Times Magazine*, January 23, 1994; U.N. Department of Humanitarian Affairs, op. cit. note 10.

28. Inadequacy of available funds from HRW and PHR, op. cit. note 26; Kuwait from Paul Lewis, "Red Cross to Urge U.N. to Adopt a Complete Ban on Land Mines," *New York Times*, February 28, 1994; peacekeeping-related demining spending from Patrick Blagden, U.N. Department of Peace-Keeping Operations, New York, private communication, May 3, 1994, and from Patrick M. Blagden, Statement before Landmine Hearing, op. cit. note 26; total U.N. spending from David Gowdey, U.N. Department of Humanitarian Affairs, New York, private communication, September 1, 1994. Central America from Ricardo Gjivoje, Organisation of American States, Washington, D.C., private communication, May 3, 1994.

29. Afghanistan from U.N. Department of Humanitarian Affairs, *DHA News*, September-December 1993; Cambodia from HRW and PHR, op. cit. note 26; Mozambique from Ball, op. cit. note 24.

30. Lack of breakthrough in developing improved mine clearance techniques from Boutros Boutros-Ghali, Statement before Landmine Hearing, op. cit. note 26; progress of campaign for landmine ban from Robert O. Muller, Executive Director, Vietnam Veterans of America Foundation, Statement before Landmine Hearing, op. cit. note 26; export moratoria from U.N. General Assembly, op. cit. note 26; German budget from "Weltweite Ächtung von Landminen Gefordert," *E+Z - Entwicklung und Zusammenarbeit*, April 1994.

31. John Darnton, "U.N. Faces Refugee Crisis That Never Ends," *New York Times*, August 8, 1994; Hal Kane, "Refugee Flows Swelling," in Brown, Kane, and Roodman, op. cit. note 7.

32. Figure for 1988 from reports issued by U.N. General Assembly, Executive Committee of the High Commissioner's Programme, "Overview of UNHCR Activities. Report for 1988-1989," August 25, 1989, and "Voluntary Funds Administered by the UNHCR. Accounts for the Year 1988 and Report of the Board of Auditors Thereon," July 18, 1989; figure for 1993 from Heather Courtney, Public Information Assistant, UNHCR, U.S. Branch Office, Washington, D.C., private communication, May 25, 1994; figure for 1994 projection and Jessen-Petersen quote from Paul Lewis, "Agency Hopes for Fall in Number of Refugees," *New York Times*, March 20, 1994.

33. Table 5 based on Alvaro de Soto and Graciana del Castillo, "Obstacles to Peacebuilding," *Foreign Policy*, Number 94, Spring 1994, for overview; Guatemala from "FONAPAZ 1993 Annual Report," "FONAPAZ: The Reason for its Existence," and "FONAPAZ and the Communities: Building Peace" (information brochures), Fondo Nacional para la Paz, Presidency of the Republic of Guatemala, undated; El Salvador from Gabriel Aguilera, "Problems of Military Demobilization in Central America," *Cuadernos de Trabajo*, No. 14, Arias Foundation for Peace and Human Progress, San José, Costa Rica, July 1993, from United Nations, "Report of the Secretary-General on the United Nations Observer Mission in El Salvador," 11 May 1994, and from GAO, *El Salvador: Status of Reconstruction Activities One Year After the Peace Agreement* (Gaithersburg, Md., 1993); Haiti from U.N. Daily Highlights Press Release DH/1734, September 21, 1994; Mozambique from United Nations, "Report of the Secretary-General on the United Nations Operation in Mozambique," July 7, 1994, and from Mark C. Chona and Jeffrey I. Herbst, "Southern Africa," in Anthony Lake et al., *After the Wars: Reconstruction in Afghanistan, Indochina, Central America, Southern Africa, and the Horn of Africa* (New Brunswick, N.J.: Transaction Publishers for Overseas Development Council, 1990); South Africa from Jenny Cargill, "Südafrikas Teure Demokratie," *Der Überblick*, June 1994, and from Bill Keller, "Mandela's First 100 Days: `On Course,' He Says," *New York Times*, August 19, 1994; Palestine from Thomas L. Friedman, "Agency Offering an Aid Blueprint for Palestinians," *New York Times*, May 3, 1994, from Youssef M. Ibrahim, "P.L.O. Pleads for Faster Disbursement of Foreign Aid Money," *New York Times*, June 10, 1994, from Alan Riding, "Palestinians Given Pledges For More Aid," *New York Times*, June 11, 1994, from Youssef M. Ibrahim, "Israeli-P.L.O. Squabble Delays Aid for Arabs," *New York Times*, September 10, 1994, and from "UNRWA: Supporting the Peace," *Palestine Refugees Today*, January 1994; Kuwait from GAO, *Persian Gulf: U.S. Business Participation in the Reconstruction of Kuwait* (Gaithersburg, Md., 1992), from Cory Wright, U.S. Department of Commerce, Washington, D.C., private communication, August 9, 1994, and from Institute for Defense and Disarmament Studies (IDDS), Arms Control Reporter 1994 (Cambridge, Massachusetts: IDDS, 1994), sheet 453. B-1.29; Bosnia from United Nations, "Pledging Conference to Raise Funds for Restoration of Essential Services to Sarajevo, to be Held in New York on 29 June," Press Release, New York, June 24, 1994. Arias quote from Oscar Arias Sánchez, "Peace and Security in Central America," in Aguilar Urbina, op. cit. note 20.

34. Tufts, op. cit. note 18.

35. UNDP, Office for Project Services (OPS), Linking Rehabilitation and Development: Managing Revitalization of War-Torn Areas, undated brochure; UNDP, OPS, "CARERE: An Area Development Programme," undated brochure.

36. Enrique Neuhauser, Senior Adviser, UNDP, Regional Bureau for Latin America and the Caribbean, New York, private communication, September 14, 1994; UNDP, op. cit. note 2, Box 3.3: "A Central American Accord for Human Development"; UNDP, OPS, "PRODERE—Development Programme for Displaced Persons, Refugees and Returnees in Central America," undated set of brochures; Jean Christophe Bouvier, Senior Programme Management Officer, UNDP, OPS, New York, private communication, September 20, 1994.

37. Project funding from Oscar Yujnovsky, UNDP, Regional Bureau for Latin America and the Caribbean, New York, private communication, October 20, 1994, and from Bouvier, op. cit. note 36. Details are discussed in ACNUR/UNDP, "Estado del financiamento y localizacion de los proyectos CIREFCA y de otras iniciativas en el marco de CIREFCA," internal document, San José, Costa Rica, February 1993. Per-beneficiary spending from UNDP, OPS, op. cit. note 36; per capita military spending from ACDA, *World Military Expenditures and Arms Transfers 1991-1992* (Washington, D.C.: U.S. Government Printing Office, March 1994).

38. World Bank, op. cit. note 21; Jürgen Brauer and Domenick Bertelli, "Passing the Buck: International Banks and Aid for Conversion," *CEP Research Report*, January 1994; Colletta, op. cit. note 18.

39. De Soto and del Castillo, op. cit. note 33; Liisa L. North, "The Challenge of Demobilization: The Construction of Peace and Regional Security," in Aguilar Urbina, op. cit. note 20.

40. De Soto and del Castillo, op. cit. note 33; Anthony Lake, "After the Wars--What *Kind* of Peace?" in Lake, op. cit. note 33.

41. $5 trillion estimate from William Arkin and Robert S. Norris, "The Nuclear Follies, Post-Cold War," in Ruth Leger Sivard, *World Military and Social Expenditures 1993* (Washington, D.C.: World Priorities, 1993); projected savings from Congressional Budget Office, *The START Treaty and Beyond* (Washington, D.C.: October 1991), and from CBO, *Implementing START II*, CBO Papers (Washington, D.C.: March 1993).

42. Cost classification from Tom Troyano, Department of Defense, Office of the Secretary of Defense, Office of Strategy, Arms Control, and Compliance, Washington, D.C., private communication, August 1, 1994. Submarine decommissioning from Captain F.G. Leeder, Deputy Chief of Information, Department of the Navy, Office of Information, Washington, D.C., private communication,

May 6, 1994. Air Force costs are a Worldwatch calculation based on Major Cindy Scott-Johnson, Air Force Public Affairs, Media Relations Division, Washington, D.C., private communication, September 30, 1994. B-1B and Minuteman III costs from IDDS 1994, op. cit. note 33, sheet 611.E-0.1.

43. Warhead dismantlement rate and costs estimate from OTA, op. cit. note 16; plutonium storage costs from David Rohde, "Disposal of Warhead Plutonium Awaits Federal Study of Options," *Christian Science Monitor*, June 14, 1994; disposal cost estimates from C.H. Bloomster et al., "Options and Regulatory Issues Related to Disposition of Fissile Materials from Arms Reduction," Pacific Northwest Laboratory, Richland, Washington, December 1990, prepared for the U.S. Department of Energy, presented at the Annual Meeting of the American Association for the Advancement of Science, Washington, D.C., February 18, 1991, and from Nuclear Safety Campaign, *Beyond the Bomb: Dismantling Nuclear Weapons and Disposing of their Radioactive Wastes* (Seattle: January 1994).

44. Russian costs from Alexei Arbatov, ed., *Implications of the START II Treaty for US-Russian Relations*, Report No. 9 (Washington, D.C.: Henry L. Stimson Center, October 1993); Ukraine from Elaine Sciolino, "Ukraine Missiles: Terms Are Tough," *New York Times*, October 26, 1993; Kazakhstan from IDDS 1994, op. cit. note 33, sheet 611.E-3.94.

45. IDDS 1994, op. cit. note 33, sheets 611.E-4.6 and -4.7.

46. Initial plans from Frances Williams, "Hopes High for International Chemical Weapons Treaty," *Financial Times*, August 26, 1992; staff of 365 from Anil Wadhwa, "The Preparatory Phase of Setting up the Organisation for the Prohibition of Chemical Weapons," *Disarmament. A Periodic Review by the United Nations*, Vol. XVI, No. 3 (1993); Kenyon from IDDS, *Arms Control Reporter 1993* (Cambridge, Mass: IDDS, 1993), sheet 704.B.558; 1994 and 1995 budgets from Serguei B. Batsanov, Director for External Relations, Preparatory Commission for the Organisation for the Prohibition of Chemical Weapons, Provisional Technical Secretariat, The Hague, Netherlands, private communication, April 7, 1994; 1994 budget request from Keir A. Lieber, "Highlights of the Fifth PrepCom Plenary," *The CWC Chronicle* (Henry L. Stimson Center), January 1994; expected annual inspection costs from *Pacific Research*, February 1994; threat to OPCW's capability from "Editor's Note," *The CWC Chronicle*, January 1994.

47. Destruction-to-production cost ratio from J.P. Perry Robinson, Thomas Stock, and Ronald G. Sutherland, "The Chemical Weapons Convention: The Success of Chemical Disarmament Negotiations," in SIPRI, *SIPRI Yearbook 1993: World Armaments and Disarmament* (New York: Oxford University Press, 1993). Yeltsin from IDDS 1993, op. cit. note 46, sheet 704.B.552.

48. U.S. costs from Thomas Stock and Anna De Geer, "Chemical Weapon Developments," in SIPRI 1994, op. cit. note 5; buried ammunition cost from U.S. Department of the Army, Non-Stockpile Chemical Materiel Program, *Survey and Analysis Report* (U.S. Army Chemical Materiel Destruction Agency, Program Manager for Non-Stockpile Chemical Materiel, November 1993); annual funding from Tischbin, op. cit. note 14.

49. 1997 starting date and foreign aid need from Stock and De Geer, op. cit. note 48, and from IDDS 1993, op. cit. note 46, sheet 704.E-2.106; explosives charge factor from GAO, *Arms Control: Status of U.S.-Russian Agreements and the Chemical Weapons Convention*, GAO/NSIAD-94-136 (Gaithersburg, MD: March 1994); cost estimate from Serguei Kisselev, Deputy Head of the Delegation of the Russian Federation to the Preparatory Commission for the Organization for the Prohibition of Chemical Weapons, Embassy of the Russian Federation, The Hague, Netherlands, private communication, July 10, 1994 (his estimate does not include the cost of destroying production facilities).

50. German spending from *Bundeshaushaltsplan 1994*, op. cit. note 17 (and earlier volumes), and from "Stand der Bewirtschaftung HH-Einnahmen/-Ausgaben, Endergebnis des BMF," Haushaltsjahr 1993, Kapitel 1409, computer printout, German Ministry of Finance, February 16, 1994, as provided by the Press Office of the German Defense Ministry, Bonn, July 20, 1994. The spending figure represents actual expenditures for 1991-1993 and appropriations for 1994. U.S. spending from GAO, *Conventional Arms Control: Former Warsaw Pact Nations' Treaty Compliance and U.S. Cost Control*, GAO/NSIAD-94-33 (Gaithersburg, MD: December 1993). Other NATO countries from Duncan, op. cit. note 17, from Vester, op. cit. note 14, from Stokes, op. cit. note 15, from Fisas Armengol, op. cit. note 16, and from private communications with Lt. Col. Christian Schmitt, Military Attache's office, Embassy of Denmark, Washington, D.C., July 25, 1994, with Lorraine Sanda, CFE Desk, British Foreign and Commonwealth Office, London, July 27, 1994, and with Donald Banks, Canadian Department of Foreign Affairs, Non-Proliferation, Arms Control, and Disarmament Division, Ottawa, July 28, 1994.

51. Limited resources from GAO, op. cit. note 50, and from IDDS 1994, op. cit. note 33, sheets 407.B.505 and -.506; Czech spending from Directorate for Press, Information and Public Relations of the Ministry of Defense of the Czech Republic, *1994 Army of the Czech Republic* (Prague, 1994); Belarus from IDDS 1994, op. cit. note 33, sheet 407.B.508; Russian preference to let tanks rust from Steven Miller, Editor, *International Security*, Cambridge, Massachusetts, private communication, August 15, 1994.

52. Global disposal market estimate from Adam Bryant, "Venture Hopes to Cash in on Military Cutbacks," *New York Times*, June 23, 1992; tonnage demilitarized from "Army Looks for Ways to Reuse, Recycle Munitions," *Environmental Update. A Quarterly Publication of Army Environmental News*, October 1993; expenditures from John McCoy, U.S. Army Materiel Command, Alexandria, Virginia, private communication, August 26, 1994; ammunition production capacity funding requests from GAO, *1994 Defense Budget: Potential Reductions to Ammunition Programs*, GAO/NSIAD-93-296 (Gaithersburg, MD: September 20, 1993), and from Thomas E. Ricks, "A Post-Cold War Defense Plan Maps a Smaller But Ready Force," *Wall Street Journal*, February 28, 1994; ammunition procurement appropriations from procurement section of Department of Defense Appropriations Acts, 1990-1994.

53. Russian budget allocation from Ksenia Gonchar, IMEMO Institute, Moscow, private communication, October 6, 1994. Sources for Table 6: ACDA from William Amoroso, Budget Office, U.S. Arms Control and Disarmament Agency, Washington, D.C., private communication, January 11, 1994; OSIA from Major Mock, U.S. On-Site Inspection Agency, Public Affairs Office, Washington, D.C., private communication, January 6, 1994; INF from GAO, op. cit. note 17; START from Leeder and Scott-Johnson, both op. cit. note 43; CFE from GAO, op. cit. note 50; chemical weapons-related costs from GAO, op. cit. note 49, and from Tischbin, op. cit. note 14; DOE Nuclear Verification and Control Technology from Jeff Andrews, Department of Energy, Public Affairs Office, Washington, D.C., private communication, October 4, 1994, and from Department of Energy, Office of the Chief Financial Officer, *FY 1995 Budget Highlights* (Washington, D.C: National Technical Information Service, February 1994); ammunition disposal from McCoy, op. cit. note 52; base closure from U.S. Department of Defense, *FY 1995 Budget Estimates: DoD Base Realignment and Closure. Justification Data Submitted to Congress*, Washington, D.C., February 1994; conversion from "Defense Reinvestment and Conversion," *The New Economy*, Winter 1994, and from Greg Bischak, Executive Director, National Commission for Economic Conversion and Disarmament, Washington, D.C., private communication, August 11, 1994.

54. Mid-1980s figure from Michael Renner, *Economic Adjustments After the Cold War: Strategies for Conversion* (Aldershot, England: Dartmouth Publishing Co., 1992); 1980s losses from Michael Renner, "Disarmament, Arms Conversion, and the Environment," *Calypso Log*, June 1992; projection to 1998 from Herbert Wulf, "Arms Industry Limited: The Turning-Point in the 1990s," in Herbert Wulf, ed., *Arms Industry Limited* (New York: Oxford University Press, 1993); demobilization figures from Wulf, op. cit. note 3.

55. U.S. base closure decision-making process is detailed in Center for Economic Conversion, *Base Conversion News*, Winter 1991. The German government does not maintain data that would allow a calculation of costs and savings associated with base closures. Dr. Hoyer, Bundesministerium der Verteidigung, Referat H II 5, Bonn, Germany, private communication, October 13, 1994. The United Kingdom is only beginning to undertake significant base closures. Col. Jiggens, Chief of Staff, Directorate of Base Depots, British Army, private communication, September 12, 1994.

56. Previous closures from Tyrus W. Cobb, "Close the Bases—Now," *Washington Post*, June 1, 1994; projected costs and savings from DOD, op. cit. note 53; U.S. overseas base closures from "US to Cut Military Facilities in Europe," *Financial Times*, June 17, 1994.

57. Wulf, op. cit. note 3.

58. Early funding from Maggie Bierwirth, "Capitol Hill and Conversion: A Summary of Recent Congressional Action," in Kevin J. Cassidy and Gregory A. Bischak, eds., *Real Security. Converting the Defense Economy and Building Peace* (Albany: State University of New York Press, 1993); 1994-97 figures are detailed in "Defense Reinvestment and Conversion," op. cit. note 53.

59. Buchanan quoted in Greg Bischak, "Military Tightens Grip on 1995 Defense Budget; Modest Conversion Gains in Question," *The New Economy*, Spring 1994; Robyn quoted in Randy Barrett, "Conversion Confusion," *Technology Transfer Business*, Fall 1994; civilian share of TRP from Bischak, op. cit. note 53.

60. Michael Oden, "Dual-Use or Doublespeak?," *Positive Alternatives*, Winter 1994; Bischak, op. cit. note 59; Bierwirth, op. cit. note 58.

61. Lack of conversion budget in Spain from Fisas Armengol, op. cit. note 16, and in Britain from Adrian Kendry, "The Defense Budget and Defense Employment in the UK: Iceberg Effect for the Supply Chain," *The New Economy*, Spring 1994; Italy from Mario Pianta, National Research Council, Rome, Italy, private communication, August 1, 1994, and from John Simkins, "Italy Announces Plan to Reshape and Boost State Defence Industry," *Financial Times*, March 11, 1994; France from Ian Anthony et al., "Arms Production and Arms Trade," in SIPRI 1994, op. cit. note 5.

62. Wulf, op. cit. note 20; further, see Renner, op. cit. note 54.

63. Brandenburg from Johann Peter, Arbeitsstab des Bevollmächtigten des Ministerpräsidenten für die Westgruppe der Streitkräfte und Konversion, Land Brandenburg, Potsdam, Germany, private communication, August 2, 1994; Rheinland-Pfalz from Christian Wellmann, "Abrüstung und Beschäftigung—ein Zielkonflikt?," *Gewerkschaftliche Monatshefte*, August 1989; compensation budget from *Bundeshaushaltsplan 1994*, op. cit. note 17 and from "Stand der Bewirtschaftung HH-Einnahmen/-Ausgaben, Endergebnis des BMF," op. cit. note 50.

64. "European Commission Addresses Conversion," *The New Economy*, Summer 1993; Les Verts au Parlement Européen, Groupe de Travail "Paix et Disarmament", *Vers une Nouvelle Politique de Sécurité, Non-Prolifération, Essais Nucléaires, Industries d'Armements, Commerce des Armes, Objection de Conscience, Ex-Yugoslavie* (Brussels, undated); Herbert Wulf, Director, Bonn International Center for Conversion, private communication, October 14, 1994.

65. "Sonderkredit für Abrüstung in Entwicklungsländern," *E+Z*, Vol. 35, No. 8 (1994); Anthony et al., op. cit. note 61; Wulf, op. cit. note 64. Philippines from UNDP, op. cit. note 2.

66. Liu Yumin, "Conversion in China," *Press for Conversion!*, Issue #17, May 1994; Nicole Ball et al., "World Military Expenditure," in SIPRI 1994, op. cit. note 5.

67. Yudit [sic] Kiss, "The Pains of Defense Industry Conversion in East Central Europe," *The New Economy*, Spring 1994; Oldrich Cechak, Jan Selesovsky, and Milan Stembera, "Czechoslovakia: Reductions in Arms Production in a Time of Economic and Political Transformation," in Wulf, op. cit. note 54.

68. Unfulfilled conversion plans from David W. McFadden, "Post-Soviet Conversion: Problems and Prospects," in Cassidy and Bischak, op. cit. note 58; military equipment decrease from Igor Khripunov, "Delusions vs. Conversion," *Bulletin of the Atomic Scientists*, July/August 1994; Russian conversion cost estimates from Alexei Izyumov, "The Soviet Union: Arms Control and Conversion-Plan and Reality," in Wulf, op. cit. note 54; limited capacity to pay for conversion from Saadet Deger, "World Military Expenditure," in SIPRI 1993, op. cit. note 47.

69. Gonchar, op. cit. note 53; Khripunov, op. cit. note 68; Julian Cooper, Director, Centre for Russian and East European Studies, University of Birmingham, United Kingdom, private communication, October 3, 1994.

70. Khripunov, op. cit. note 68; re-emerging arms export emphasis from Ball et al., op. cit. note 66.

71. Number of troops and dependents from Stephen Kinzer, "Russian Troops Bid `Wiedersehen' to Germany," *New York Times*, September 1, 1994; Grachev from Ball et al., op. cit. note 66; German payments from "Leistungen nach dem Überleitungsabkommen, Stand Februar 1994," unpublished printout, as provided by Mr. Reim, German Finance Ministry, Bonn, Germany, private communication, August 23, 1994. The 1991-95 total is composed of actual expenditures (1991-93), budget appropriations (1994), and projections (1995).

72. Chemical disarmament from GAO, op. cit. note 49, and from IDDS 1993, op. cit. note 46; nuclear disarmament aid from IDDS 1993, op. cit. note 46, and from IDDS, *Arms Control Reporter 1992* (Cambridge, Mass.: IDDS, 1992), section 611.E-3.

73. "U.S. Helps Former Soviet Union Reduce Threat," News Release, U.S. Department of Defense, Office of Assistant Secretary of Defense (Public Affairs),, Washington, D.C., March 15, 1994; "Semi-Annual Report on Program Activities to Facilitate Weapons Destruction and Nonproliferation in the Former Soviet Union," Washington, D.C., April 30, 1994, submitted by U.S. Secretary of Defense, William J. Perry, to Thomas S. Foley, Speaker of the House of Representatives and to Albert Gore, Jr., President of the Senate, on May 14, 1994; U.S. Department of Defense, Defense Nuclear Agency, private communication, August 8, 1994.

74. IDDS 1994, op. cit. note 33, sheet 611.E-3.90.

75. Worldwatch calculations based on Organisation for Economic Co-operation and Development (OECD), Centre for Co-Operation with Economies in Transition (CCET), "CCET Register Projects in the Defence Conversion Sector," CCET Register Report #0071, Paris (as of February 22, 1994). A request for an updated version of the register was denied: officially, access is restricted to governments and multilateral institutions; OECD might allow nongovernmental organizations, universities, and private-sector access in the future, but as of August 1994 no such decision was imminent. Jean Gomm, Principal Administrator, CCET, Paris, private communication, August 8, 1994.

76. Brauer and Bertelli, op. cit. note 38; European Bank for Reconstruction and Development, "Russia: Military Conversion Programme," Presentation to the European Parliament Committee on Military Conversion, April 28/29, 1993.

77. TACIS funds from Christina Thormählen, European Commission, Directorate General I, External Economic Relations, TACIS Information Office, Brussels, Belgium, private communication, August 3, 1994; U.S. funds from "Funds for Russian Defense Conversion," in: "Flashfax BISNIS Bank" (24-hour automated fax delivery system), U.S. Department of Commerce, International Trade Administration, Business Information Service for the Newly Independent States, Washington, D.C., dated February 4, 1994; Perry quote from "Semi-Annual Report on Program Activities to Facilitate Weapons Destruction and Nonproliferation in the Former Soviet Union," op. cit. note 73.

78. Fees to Western consultants from Brooks Tigner, "Europeans Push Conversion in Russia," *Press for Conversion!*, Issue #17, May 1994, from Khripunov, op. cit. note 68, and from Domenick Bertelli, Council on Economic Priorities, "DoD to review conversion aid to NI. Shakeup in Russian aid program may be on the way," Feb 16, 1994, as posted on igc:econ.conversion on Econet electronic conference bulletin board, based on a preliminary study ordered by Graham Allison, U.S. Assistant Secretary of Defense for Policy and Plans; Russian resentment and Lugar quote from Adi Ignatius, "U.S. Stirs Russian Resentment With Plans for Defense Conversion," *Wall Street Journal*, September 19, 1994.

79. For a discussion of the growth of peacekeeping and the proposal for early-warning capabilities, see Michael Renner, *Critical Juncture: The Future of Peacekeeping*, Worldwatch Paper 114 (Washington, D.C.: Worldwatch Institute, May 1993); peacekeeping expenditures from Amir Dossal, Field Finance and Budget Section, Field Operations Division, Department of Peace-keeping Operations, United Nations, New York, private communications, February 14 and September 15, 1994.

80. Security Council committees from Paul Lewis, "U.N. Is Worried by Human Cost of Embargoes," *New York Times*, December 19, 1993. Lloyd J. Dumas, "Sanctions: Organizing the Chaos," *Bulletin of the Atomic Scientists*, November 1993, presents a detailed proposal for a U.N. sanctions council.

81. Macedonia losses from Saso Ordanoski, "Balkan Stepchild" (op-ed), *New York Times*, September 4, 1994; deadlock over support fund from "U.N. Sanctions Fund to Shield the Innocent Opposed," *Development Hotline*, August 1993.

82. Number of U.N. electoral missions from U.N. Daily Highlights Press Release DH/1712, August 19, 1994; further, see Robin A. Ludwig, "Gefragt Wie Nie Zuvor," and Larry Garber, "Eher Kunst als Wissenschaft," both in *Der Überblick*, March 1993.

83. Ludwig, op. cit. note 82; Robin A. Ludwig, Electoral Assistance Division, U.N. Department of Political Affairs, New York, private communication, August 15, 1994; Swedish initiative from Bengt Säve-Söderbergh, "Wachsamkeit von Anfang an," *Der Überblick*, March 1993.

84. International Court of Justice, *Yearbook 1991-1992* (The Hague, Netherlands, 1992), Chapter VII: "Finances of the Court"; Arthur Th. Witteveen, Secretary in charge of information matters, International Court of Justice, The Hague, Netherlands, private communication, May 18, 1994.

85. "Status of the International Criminal Court (ICC): July 1994," World Federalist Association factsheet, Washington, D.C., undated.

86. Ibid.; Richard D. Lyons, "U.N. Approves Tribunal on Rwandan Atrocities," *New York Times*, November 9, 1994; Jane Perlez, "U.N. Rwanda Rights Effort is Hurt by Understaffing," *New York Times*, August 25, 1994.

87. "Status of the International Criminal Court (ICC): July 1994," op. cit. note 85; U.N. Information Service, "International Law Commission Concludes Forty-Sixth Session, Geneva, 3 May - 22 July," Press Release L/2684, Geneva, July 25, 1994; U.N. Daily Highlights Press Releases DH/1640, 9 May 1994 and DH/1691, 21 July 1994.

88. Some of these issues are explored in Jeffrey H. Grotte and Julia L. Klare, *Balancing Cost and Effectiveness in Arms Control Monitoring*, IDA Paper P-2756 (Alexandria, Virginia: Institute for Defense Analyses, September 1992), and in CBO, op. cit. note 17.

89. Worldwatch calculations based on U.N. Department for Disarmament Affairs, Disarmament Study Series No. 9, *The Implications of Establishing an International Satellite Monitoring Agency* (New York: 1983).

90. Barry M. Blechman and J. Matthew Vaccaro, *Training for Peacekeeping: The United Nations' Role*, Occasional Papers Series, Report No. 12 (Washington, D.C.: Henry L. Stimson Center, 1994). The Canadian government has decided to establish a national peacekeeping training centre at a former military base in Nova Scotia. Department of National Defence, Backgrounder, "Cornwallis: A Canadian International Peacekeeping Training Centre," Ottawa, Canada, February 1994. The Scandinavian countries and some other nations have established national training courses and facilities that, to varying degrees, are open to nationals from foreign countries.

91. Peacekeeping arrears from various U.N. "Daily Highlights" press releases published during 1994.

92. Oscar Arias Sánchez, "A Global Demilitarization Fund," special contribution to UNDP, op. cit. note 2. The proposals discussed in this section have in part been developed in a series of informal consultations in January and February 1994, via e-mail, with staff at the Center for Peace and Reconciliation, Arias Foundation for Peace and Human Progress in San José, Costa Rica.

93. Arias Sánchez, op. cit. note 92.

94. Worldwatch calculation based on projected military expenditures and military budget savings in Table 3.1. of UNDP, op. cit. note 2.

95. Official development assistance (ODA) made available by members of the OECD amounted to $54.8 billion in 1993, or 0.29 percent of OECD member states' GNP- -the lowest ratio reported since 1973. Moreover, since the late 1970s and early 1980s, the share of ODA allotted to U.N. agencies and other multilateral institutions declined. See U.N. Press Release, op. cit. note 10.

96. Ball, op. cit. note 24.

PUBLICATION ORDER FORM

No. of
Copies

_____ 57. **Nuclear Power: The Market Test** by Christopher Flavin.

_____ 58. **Air Pollution, Acid Rain, and the Future of Forests** by Sandra Postel.

_____ 60. **Soil Erosion: Quiet Crisis in the World Economy** by Lester R. Brown and Edward C. Wolf.

_____ 61. **Electricity's Future: The Shift to Efficiency and Small-Scale Power** by Christopher Flavin.

_____ 63. **Energy Productivity: Key to Environmental Protection and Economic Progress** by William U. Chandler.

_____ 65. **Reversing Africa's Decline** by Lester R. Brown and Edward C. Wolf.

_____ 66. **World Oil: Coping With the Dangers of Success** by Christopher Flavin.

_____ 67. **Conserving Water: The Untapped Alternative** by Sandra Postel.

_____ 68. **Banishing Tobacco** by William U. Chandler.

_____ 69. **Decommissioning: Nuclear Power's Missing Link** by Cynthia Pollock.

_____ 70. **Electricity For A Developing World: New Directions** by Christopher Flavin.

_____ 71. **Altering the Earth's Chemistry: Assessing the Risks** by Sandra Postel.

_____ 75. **Reassessing Nuclear Power: The Fallout From Chernobyl** by Christopher Flavin.

_____ 77. **The Future of Urbanization: Facing the Ecological and Economic Constraints** by Lester R. Brown and Jodi L. Jacobson.

_____ 78. **On the Brink of Extinction: Conserving The Diversity of Life** by Edward C. Wolf.

_____ 79. **Defusing the Toxics Threat: Controlling Pesticides and Industrial Waste** by Sandra Postel.

_____ 80. **Planning the Global Family** by Jodi L. Jacobson.

_____ 81. **Renewable Energy: Today's Contribution, Tomorrow's Promise** by Cynthia Pollock Shea.

_____ 82. **Building on Success: The Age of Energy Efficiency** by Christopher Flavin and Alan B. Durning.

_____ 83. **Reforesting the Earth** by Sandra Postel and Lori Heise.

_____ 84. **Rethinking the Role of the Automobile** by Michael Renner.

_____ 86. **Environmental Refugees: A Yardstick of Habitability** by Jodi L. Jacobson.

_____ 88. **Action at the Grassroots: Fighting Poverty and Environmental Decline** by Alan B. Durning.

_____ 89. **National Security: The Economic and Environmental Dimensions** by Michael Renner.

_____ 90. **The Bicycle: Vehicle for a Small Planet** by Marcia D. Lowe.

_____ 91. **Slowing Global Warming: A Worldwide Strategy** by Christopher Flavin

_____ 92. **Poverty and the Environment: Reversing the Downward Spiral** by Alan B. Durning.

_____ 93. **Water for Agriculture: Facing the Limits** by Sandra Postel.

_____ 94. **Clearing the Air: A Global Agenda** by Hilary F. French.

_____ 95. **Apartheid's Environmental Toll** by Alan B. Durning.

_____ 96. **Swords Into Plowshares: Converting to a Peace Economy** by Michael Renner.

_____ 97. **The Global Politics of Abortion** by Jodi L. Jacobson.

_____ 98. **Alternatives to the Automobile: Transport for Livable Cities** by Marcia D. Lowe.

_____ 99. **Green Revolutions: Environmental Reconstruction in Eastern Europe and the Soviet Union** by Hilary F. French.

_____100. **Beyond the Petroleum Age: Designing a Solar Economy** by Christopher Flavin and Nicholas Lenssen.

_____101. **Discarding the Throwaway Society** by John E. Young.

_____102. **Women's Reproductive Health: The Silent Emergency** by Jodi L. Jacobson.

_____103. **Taking Stock: Animal Farming and the Environment** by Alan B. Durning and Holly B. Brough.

_____104. **Jobs in a Sustainable Economy** by Michael Renner.

_____105. **Shaping Cities: The Environmental and Human Dimensions** by Marcia D. Lowe.

_____106. **Nuclear Waste: The Problem That Won't Go Away** by Nicholas Lenssen.

_____107. **After the Earth Summit: The Future of Environmental Governance**
        by Hilary F. French.
_____108. **Life Support: Conserving Biological Diversity** by John C. Ryan.
_____109. **Mining the Earth** by John E. Young.
_____110. **Gender Bias: Roadblock to Sustainable Development** by Jodi L. Jacobson.
_____111. **Empowering Development: The New Energy Equation** by Nicholas Lenssen.
_____112. **Guardians of the Land: Indigenous Peoples and the Health of the Earth**
        by Alan Thein Durning.
_____113. **Costly Tradeoffs: Reconciling Trade and the Environment** by Hilary F. French.
_____114. **Critical Juncture: The Future of Peacekeeping** by Michael Renner.
_____115. **Global Network: Computers in a Sustainable Society** by John E. Young.
_____116. **Abandoned Seas: Reversing the Decline of the Oceans** by Peter Weber.
_____117. **Saving the Forests: What Will It Take?** by Alan Thein Durning.
_____118. **Back on Track: The Global Rail Revival** by Marcia D. Lowe.
_____119. **Powering the Future: Blueprint for a Sustainable Electricity Industry**
        by Christopher Flavin and Nicholas Lenssen.
_____120. **Net Loss: Fish, Jobs, and the Marine Environment** by Peter Weber.
_____121. **The Next Efficiency Revolution: Creating a Sustainable Materials Economy**
        by John E. Young and Aaron Sachs.
_____122. **Budgeting for Disarmament: The Costs of War and Peace** by Michael Renner.
_____ **Total Copies**

☐ **Single Copy: $5.00**
☐ **Bulk Copies (any combination of titles)**
    ☐ 2–5: $4.00 ea.   ☐ 6–20: $3.00 ea.   ☐ 21 or more: $2.00 ea.
    Inquire for discounts on larger orders.
☐ **Membership in the Worldwatch Library: $30.00 (international airmail $45.00)**
    The paperback edition of our 250-page "annual physical of the planet,"
    State of the World, plus all Worldwatch Papers released during the calendar year.
☐ **Subscription to *World Watch* Magazine: $20.00 (international airmail $35.00)**
    Stay abreast of global environmental trends and issues with our award-
    winning, eminently readable bimonthly magazine.

☐ **Worldwatch Database Disk: $89**
Includes up-to-the-minute global agricultural, energy, economic, environmental, social,
and military indicators from all current Worldwatch publications.

Please check one: _____high-density IBM-compatible or   _____Macintosh
---

Please include $3 postage and handling for non-subscription orders.

Make check payable to Worldwatch Institute
1776 Massachusetts Avenue, N.W., Washington, D.C. 20036-1904 USA

Enclosed is my check for U.S. $_____

VISA ☐   MasterCard ☐   _____
                                    Card Number   Expiration Date

_____
name   **daytime phone #**

_____
address

_____
city   **state**   **zip/country**
Phone: (202) 452-1999   Fax: (202) 296-7365   E-Mail: wwpub@igc.apc.org